CULTURE, EDUCATION AND CREATIVITY

Culture, Education and Creativity

(A study of Anxiety and Creative Potential)

B. S. Dagar
Reader
Department of Education
M.D. University, Rohtak (Haryana)

Foreword by
Professor G. Ram Reddy
Vice-Chancellor
Indira Gandhi National Open University,
New Delhi-110016

Uppal Publishing House
NEW DELHI-110002

UPPAL PUBLISHING HOUSE
3, Ansari Road, Daryaganj, New Delhi-110002

First Edition 1989
ISBN 81-85024-46-4

Printed in India
Published by B.S. Uppal for Uppal Publishing House, New Delhi-110002 and printed at Parashar Printers, through Parashar Composing Agency, Delhi-110053

Dedicated to
My Teacher
Late Professor N.K. Dutt
As a Humble Tribute to his
Loving Memory and Everlasting Genius
Who Inspired me for pursuit of Mind

इन्दिरा गांधी राष्ट्रीय मुक्त विश्वविद्यालय

INDIRA GANDHI NATIONAL OPEN UNIVERSITY
K-76, HAUZ KHAS, NEW DELHI-110016

Prof. G. RAM REDDY
M.A. M.Sc. (London) Ph.D.
VICE-CHANCELLOR

FOREWORD

The development of the total man in tune with his own nature and also in accordance with the requirements of the physical and social environment in which he finds himself constitutes his education. Education is an ongoing process of interactions and constructions through which the individual influences the environment and in turn gets influenced by it. We educate ourselves through our volitional activities in the school and outside of it. Man continues learning even after his formal schooling is over. Even within the school hours, the child learns much more than what constitutes his curriculum.

But, is education just learning ? Does it comprise merely the acquisition of certain information, desirable habits and attitudes, and skills all that constitute what Skinner would call "shaping" of human behaviour ? No doubt, much of the human behaviour can be explained in terms of conditioning process ; but there is something that lies beyond the stimulus response and reinforcement theories, which is not banal and the common place. This aspect of human personality is termed as creativity. Man as homo sapien can be conceived in terms of his expression of this unique ability which is his exclusive prerogative.

But what is unfortunate about the educational process and practice in India and elsewhere is that, we as teachers and parents do not appreciate and recognize children who display divergent points of view. In most cases such children are even condemned. Thus, the individual who could contribute much to the cultural repertoire of human race die unknown and unsung.

In this brief but comprehensive volume the author has attempted a coherent analysis of the relationship between culture, education, and creativity. In his attempt to bring out this analysis he found the concept of anxiety deeply related to one's ability to create. Using a speculative approach, he has tried to make explicit the most controversial problem of creative thinking and mental health. In addition, the logical analysis of the concept of anxiety defining the same in comprehensive way and the treating the cause of anxiety in terms of the four types of Aristotelian causation theory is the author's original contribution.

Even as regards the empirical investigation of the problem. Dr. Dagar has delved deep by using sophisticated statistical design.

In my opinion this book will benefit scholars of psychology, sociology and education in great measures.

21.11.1988 G. RAM REDDY

PREFACE

Helping the child develop to his fullest potential is the major goal of education, especially for those who follow the "flowering seed" concept of development. Development of creative potential is the chief vehicle which results in contribution to human culture and civilization. For this aim to become a reality, we must study human personality in its different facets, especially those which are relevant to enhance creative thought expression of the child.

To the extent creativity and anxiety are the concern of education in the development of human culture, this book should prove useful. The major task of this book is three-fold :

(i) Theoretical scanning of the concept of anxiety and developing an insight into its aetiology, interpreting it basically as of three kinds—the "*moral anxiety*" the "*inferiority anxiety*" and "*separation anxiety*". The cause of the nebulous concept of anxiety has been explained in tune with four fold causation theory as initially propounded by Aristotle—viz. the *efficient cause*, the *formal cause*, the *material cause* and the *final cause*. The nomenclature given to the three types of anxiety is based upon the "formal cause" in each case. The "final cause" of anxiety comprises the most encompassing human "security base", which in turn is constituted by ones ontological freedom. That is, any apprehension which, in the last analysis, deprives one of the ontological freedom constitutes the final cause of anxiety.

(ii) Theoretical scanning of the psychodynamics of the process of creativity, especially as a conglomerate of primary and secondary process cognitions as conceived by Freud and Arieti. Effort has been made to show the possible relationship between mental health and creativity. The relationship between creativity and anxiety is perhaps still an enigma to man's understanding of it. A wide variance still exists in theoretical as well as empirical findings concerning the said relationship.

(iii) Going beyond the theoretical speculations concerning creativity, anxiety, and education vis-a-vis their impact on human culture, I have tried to make explicit the intricate relationship between anxiety (or anxiety-proneness) and creative potential empirically. In observing the relationship dimensions of human personality in terms of Eysenckian concepts of "Extraversion" "Neuroticism" and "Psychoticism" have been taken in view. For measurement of creative potential Guilford's concepts of "divergent productions" in terms of "originality", "ideational flexibility", and "fluency" were made the base. The tool used for this purpose was *Torrance Tests of Creative Thinking* (TTCT). For appraisal of the level of anxiety and anxiety-proneness, (DPI) (Dutt Personality Inventory) and "Neuroticism" scale of EPQ (Eysenek Personality Questionnaire) respectively were used.

Considering that manifest behaviour of an individual in a particular spatio-temporal context is the resultant of interactions of these factors, a complex factorial design of third order was adopted. All possible main and interaction effects were computed separately with originality, flexibility and fluency as *response* variables ; and anxiety, extraversion, psychoticism and sex constituted the *classification* variables. The same third order factorial design was adopted in another set of analyses in which anxiety was replaced by neuroticism as classification variable. It was done so because in psychological literature anxiety is conceived as a "phenotype" of which neuroticism is the "genotype". In other words, neuroticism is taken here as anxiety-proneness—a genetically determined trait of human personality. Finally a rigorous statistical design was prepared in order to obtain, what we may call, a *response surface* of creative potential. The study, thus, adopted reasonable statistical rigour with a view to reaching generalizations which warrant objectively in research.

But educational research is, as we know, a corporate activity which can not be worthwhile and complete without the involvement and cooperation of a number of individuals whose contribution in making such accomplishment a success can never be ignored. The author, therefor, is extremely grateful to all those who helped in this academic pursuit directly or indirectly.

First of all, I express my gratitude to Prof. G. Ram Reddy, the eminent educationist of international repute, and Vice-Chancellor, Indira Gandhi National Open University who very kindly has written the "Foreword" to this humble piece of research. His happy consent to write foreward and appreciation of the book is the greatest achievement for a researcher like me.

I owe a debt of gratitude to Lt. Gen. G.C. Aggarwal, Vice-Chancellors, M.D. University for his generous help and encouragement in the completion of this book.

In addition, I am extremely thankful to all those authors whose works in writing this book have been quoted by me. My sincerest thanks are due to Prof. N.K. Dutt, Prof. R.N. Mehrotra, Dr. V.K. Sabharwal and Dr. R.D. Mehta of the Department of Education, Delhi University. I am very thankful to Prof M.G. Gandhi, Prof. Tulsi Ram, and Dr. D.S. Dalal of M.D. University, Rohtak for the kind of help they rendered in the production of this book.

And finally, to my wife, Mrs. Sajjan Dagar, I owe a great deal who helped and encouraged me for bringing out this book in this shape.

B.S. Dagar
M.D. University
Rohtak (Haryana)

CONTENTS

	Foreword	
	Preface	
I	Culture, Education and Creativity	1
II	Theoretical Orientation of the Problem	19
III	Survey of Related Studies	55
IV	The Hypotheses, the Procedure and the Design of the Study	74
V	Statistical Analysis and Results	92
VI	Findings and Conclusions	130
	Bibliography	151
	Index	169

CHAPTER I

Culture, Education and Creativity

Of all the abilities that man, as 'homosapien' is endowed with, creativity is perhaps the most unique. It is creativity, as a characteristic ability of man which, among a few more, is very distinctive of him in comparison to other forms of life. Nevertheless, the other distinguishing feature which marks him uniquely from the rest of animal life is, what Arieti (1976) aptly names, "man's capacity to indulge in Aristotlian logic." Freud called this latter ability the secondary process cognition. Regarding the former ability Arieti (1976) writes :

> "Creativity is a prerogative of man, can be seen as a humble human counterpart of God's creation. The difference between the creativity of man and creation of God, according to the beliefs of some theologians and religious people, lies in the fact that whereas God's creation comes 'ex-nihilo' that is, from the spatial and temporal nothingness, human creativity is based upon what is already existing and available" (p. 4).

Distinguishing human creativity from God's creation, Hallman (1963) had also stated somewhat similarly. According to him, "human creativeness is relational . . . . man does not create the components, he can, nevertheless, create new connections among them" (Gowan et al. 1967, p. 19).

The story of man as viewed through temporal and spatial media, that is, from the most primordial man to 'homo sapien, gives an index of creativity which is uniquely human. The entire human heritage, accumulated in the form of culture and civilization, tells nothing but the story of man's endeavour to create and, thus, add to the already existing thesaurus—the store house of knowledge. And yet the fact remains that this change is the result of the efforts of a very small percentage of the potentially creative persons who lived on this planet. Who knows what would have been the picture (perhaps phenomenally different), had all potentially high creatives found chance to express their inherent powers ? Mackinnon (1962) describes the story by Mark Twain in which a person wanted to search the greatest of all generals who lived on this earth. He inquired from a number of persons. He was eventually told by St. Peter that he was a cobbler, who died. St. Peter further explained to him that had he been a general, he would have been the greatest of all of them. The essence of the story is that many great talents die unknown and unsung Had their talents been recognised and duly nurtured, they could have achieved wonders. It is, therefore, our task, as psychologists and educators, to discover talent when it is still potential and to provide the kind of social climate and intellectual environment which facilitates its nurturance and expression. It is only then that education, perhaps, can perform one of its basic functions by augmenting generation of ideas, processes, and products ; and thus gearing up the talents of pupils to the fullest possible extent.

The reality today, in this country and elsewhere as well, is something different. The curricula, the methodologies, and practices in education are so oriented that "the minds of the pupils are still treated like black boxes with informational inputs fed in at one end by the teacher, and the output tested at the other end. And the measure of quality is how well the outputs correspond to the inputs. How many teachers teach with the expectation that they can get more out of a box than they put in ?" (Suchman, 1975 p. 90).

Such a state of affairs can probably be attributed to our taking narrower view of 'giftedness' or talentedness. Students who can give best possible response to a problem, in the form of conventionally accepted best outcomes are, unequivocally, treated as highly intelligent, talented or geniuses. Deviations from conventionally accepted norms of responses are not only not valued high but are also often evaluated negatively. At times such students are labelled as eccentric, queer, bizarre or crazy. Should the uncommon student receive such a treatment from the society, either becomes neurotic or turns anti-social. Torrance (1967), in an article, "*Creative Personality and Ideal Pupil*", establishes through considerable evidence that creative personalities "tend to be estranged by their teachers and are not liked by them." Other investigators too, e.g. Getzels and Jackson (1962), Barron (1957), Mackinnon (1966) etc. are of the same opinion ; and point to the fact that teachers prefer students with high I.Q. but with less outstanding scores on test of creative thinking.

Apart from that educators hold a static and stereotyped view of intelligence (in terms of I.Q. scores), and adhere to a narrow concept of giftedness, there is yet another reason for this state of affairs. It is high academic achievement, at school or college level, that society in general and parents in particular desire and appreciate, for the simple reason that they tend to associate high academic achievement with more lucrative jobs or vocations, which in turn, they think, can and does provide security and adjustment in later life. In our society most parents desire their wards to have adjustment and security. But one must not forget the truth as Maslow (1975) asserts, "Every human being has both sets of forces within him. One set clings to safety and defensiveness out of fear (and anxiety), tending to regress, hanging on to the past, afraid to take chance, afraid to jeopardize what he already has, afraid of independence, freedom and separation. The other set of forces impels him forward toward wholeness of self and uniqueness of self, towards full functioning of all his capacities, towards confidence in the face of the external world, at the same time that he can accept his deepest, real unconscious self." Maslow views the latter set of forces as "constituting the healthy growth of an individual, a never-ending series of free choice situations, confronting each individual at every point throughout his life, in which he must choose between safety and growth, dependence and independence . . . . safety has both anxieties and delights, growth has both anxieties and delights" (Maslow, 1975, p. 109). Some people prefer the anxieties and delights of safety, while other prefer the anxieties and delights of growth. In their preference for security and adjustment some people go crazy, and they develop in themselves what Arieti (1967) would call 'adjustment syndrome'. Such people always tend to fashion their lives in such ways as to avoid any sign of mal-adjustment and insecurity. Adjustment, security and conformity become a style of life, the be-all and end-all of life. They are simply afraid of entering into anything that is new and unexplored ; feel most satisfied and happy while working in a groove. Their area of awareness shrinks, and ultimately they develop in them, what may well be called, "security-mania." Eventually, they face a thorough and complete void, meaninglessness, frustration, and anxiety, exactly what they always tended to avoid or escape.

At a stage where higher academic achievement and extreme security consciousness are the very purposes of life, we are confronted with a serious and a broader educational problem. No doubt, by following the path of conformity and commonly accepted best outcomes, academic achievement and productivity can be enhanced, but certainly we shall not create what is 'off-the-beaten-track', new, and unique. The question arises ; can it be a desirable goal of education to sacrifice uniqueness and originality to gain mass productivity and probably (pseudo) adjustment to environment ? Rogers (1959) seems to warn us correctly. He says, "unless man can make new and original adaptation to his environment, as rapidly as his science can change the environment, our culture will perish." This educational issue needs immediate consideration and decision.

What do we like our society to be ? Do we like a type of society that always tends to seek immediate adjustment in the direction of the right answers, "channelized and controlled .... where the individual appears to shy away risk and uncertainty of the unknown, and seeks safety and security of the already known ?" (Getzels and Jackson, 1975, p. 109). Or, do we like our society to become of a kind, where individuals can also venture into the unknown and the unexplored ? Most likely, a proper conglomeration of the two can be the only desired and sought-after goal of our education. Immediate adjustment, based on the security of the already known, is inconceivable as the ultimate goal of life and, hence, of education. I.Q. based concept of genius, will therefore, not be adequate if education is to contribute to the enrichment of human heritage of culture and civilization. In order that this may happen, a broader and more comprehensive view of giftedness which can include divergence and creativity will have to be accepted.

It is now clearly recognized that a frightfully large amount of human potential is being neglected. Such behaviours as originality, leadership ability, foresight, and outstanding performance in non-academic areas cannot simply be evaluated in terms of I.Q. based concept of giftedness. Moreover, the use of I.Q. as a sole criterion for determining giftedness led to the erroneous conclusion that either one is gifted or one is not. While the fact remains that people may have extremely outstanding abilities in certain area(s) while, in other they may be only mediocre or even below average. Ramanujan, the great Indian mathematician could not pass his intermediate examination and failed in all subjects—except mathematics ; but later became F.R.S. (Fellow of the Royal Society). One can write about very many such geniuses who were strong in one special area but quite below mark in others.

Towards late fifties, with the publication of *The Structure of Intellect Model* (Guilford, 1959), and the studies conducted by him and his colleagues, a new era of research opened. Guilford, in his "model of intellect", made it clear that apart from the I.Q. supported theory of giftedness, human mind is capable of divergent productions as well. The ability divergent production, if properly nurtured, may lead to creativity in the form of unique and novel products. According to Torrance (1975), Guilford proposed what was virtually tentamount to the periodic table of intellect. In his discussion of thinking as one form of the "operation" of the intellect, he talks of two types of productive thinking—convergent and divergent—which generate new information from known information and remembered information. In divergent thinking operations we think of different directions, sometimes searching, sometimes seeking variety. In convergent thinking, on the other hand, information leads to one right answer or to a recognized best or conventional answer. But creativity, as Guilford puts it, is a "many splendoured thing". Mackinnon (1962) call's it "a many faceted phenomenon", in the sense that all emotional, intellectual, cultural, and environmental aspects operate to give birth to creative insight. Let us have a brief view of what this concept means to different thinkers.

Orientalists' View of Creativity

A glimpse of the mystical and vitalistic connotation that the concept of creativity is said to be fraught with, can clearly be had in orientalists' viewpoint of creativity, especially Indian. According to Indian Philosophical view, (Chaudhury, 1975) creativeness of the highest order is effortless and spontaneous; it covers an unpredictable field of human knowledge. In the state of 'smadhi', for example, when the boundries of Ego are washed away, the distinctions of subject and object vanish, the individual is one with or merges in the ultimate reality, the Ego (aham) loses its identity and is dissolved in the universal consciousness, the Yogin at this stage enters into intuitive perception, entirely of a different nature. In this state of Yoga where there is complete 'chitta vritti nirodha', that is, cessation of the activities of the mind, extrasensory perceptions occur. Moreover, a change in the modality of consciousness takes place, and queer internal perceptions are experienced by the Yogin. This higher order creativity, according to Hindu thought, takes place when the cosmic consciousness plays upon the unperturbed individual consciousness. Jung is of the view that creativity is a function of the racial unconscious. His view somewhat agrees with the Hindu view point.

The Indian viewpoint of creativity given above is not challenged by the investigator. But, what is needed is a more workable and behavioural concept of creativity mostly followed in researches in this subject. Agreeing with Arieti (1976), the investigator wants to explicate a kind of creativity that ordinary human psyche deals with.

Occidentalists' View of Creativity

Bronowski (1958) distinguishes between discovery, invention and creativity by saying that Columbus discovered the 'West', Bell invented the 'telephone', and Shakespeare created 'Othello'. According to Bronowsky, a fact is discovered, a theory is invented but only a masterpiece is created, for, the creation must engage the whole mind. Bronowski's defiinition, however, is denotative indicating, at the same time, to what Piotrowski (1971) would call 'empirical referents' of creative product.

According to Taylor (1975), Morgan analysed twenty five earlier definitions of creativity and found that in main all these definitions point to the development of some unique product. Spearman (1931) defined it as "the power of human mind to create new content by transforming relations and thereby generating new correlates." Gestalt psychologists attempted to define creativity as an action that produces a new idea or insight through imagination rather than through reason or logic. According to McKellar (1957), creativity is the "fusion of perceptions in new ways," while Kubie defines it as "the capacity to find new connections." To Rogers (1961) it is the emergence of novel relationships ; to Murray (1959) it is new composition, and to Taylor (1975), moulding of experience into new organization. Ghiselin (1952) states creativity as the presentation of constellations of meanings. But Guilford (1962) considers that originality, which is by now said to be a necessary component of creative product, is more closely related to the personality trait of unconventionality than to the quality of newness That is, he considers originality as a function of temperament instead of objects produced (Taylor 1975).

To Thurstone (1962), in creative act there is a moment of insight ; but before that insight becomes focal there has always preceded a non-verbalized pre-focal thinking. To him the pre-focal is followed by explicit and deductive thinking before it attains the status of creative thinking. According to Arieti (1976) creativity is a process that involves a 'magic' synthesis of primary and secondary process cognitions. He calls it a tertiary process. According to associationistic thinker Mednick (1962), in creative act there occurs an association between the stimuli and responses in such a manner that the elements linked together are not normally linked. That is, S-R linkages, in such manner, seldom occur in most common people, whereas in creative people occurrence of such linkages is more or less a common place. Hebb (1949) uses the term 'serendipity' for such 'happy' combinations. According to Wallach and Kogan (1965) creativity lies in producing more associations, and in producing more that are unique.

Stein (Taylor 1975), adding slightly different dimension as social usefulness, defines creativity as a process which results in novel work that is accepted as tenable to useful or satisfying to a group of people at some point in time. MacKinon (1975) goes a step further, and attempts to define creativity as a response or an idea that is novel or at the very least, statistically infrequent, but hastens to add that novelty or originality, while a necessary aspect of creativity, is not sufficient. It must also, to some extent, be adaptive to or of reality. It must end in solution of a problem, or fit a situation, or accomplish some recognizable goal. Thirdly, 'true creativenes involves a sustaining of the original insight, an evaluation and elaboration of it—a developing of it to the full.

The brief survey made here of the various definitions of creativity indicates that different people view creativity in different perspectives. Some define the term as a product with attributes like novelty, originality etc., while other delineate it as a process which results in a unique product. Whether one conceives of creativity as a process or as a product there appears considerable divergence in them regarding definition of the concept. The reason for the same may be man's inadequacy to perceive reality in totality. The nature of the concept seems to be such that it evades a comprehensive and total view point. At this juncture, one is reminded of "Jain" interpretation of reality in Indian thought. To the question, 'What is reality' ? the Jain seers remark, 'Syad asti, Syad nasti' or 'Syad asti, nasti' (May be it is; May be, it is not) ; or "Neti, Neti," i.e. neither this is the end or that is the end. For them reality is characterized by 'anekatva' i.e. plurality or multisidedness. Attempts at defining 'creativity' appear to be similar to those at defining 'reality' in Jain philosophy. It can be viewed in a large number of perspectives and from different angles. This makes the task of evaluating various definitions of creativity, and selecting the relatively more basic one, quite difficult.

Necessary and Sufficient Conditions of Creativity

Considering such inherent difficulties in defining the concept of creativity and keeping in view the status of the available data in the form of research evidences, Hallman (1963) mentions some necessary and sufficient conditions of creativity. According to him, these conditions are a basic framework which can encompass relevant data and have predictive value too. When all these conditions are present creativity must, of necessity, result.

It would be worthwhile at this stage to take stock of what Hallman calls, necessary and sufficient conditions of creativity. This can help us get to the heart of the problem and to understand it better by developing an insight into the nature of creative process and the creative person. Hallman mentions the following five criteria which are as follows :

(1) *connectedness* ; (2) *originality* ; (3) *non-rationality* ; (4) *self-actualization* ; (5) *openness.*

The criterion of connectedness is (as Bruner, 1962 would put it) a sort of 'combinatorial activity' of the human mind. It involves the category of relations as a principle for explanation. In certain cases of artistic creativity it takes the form of metaphor, where the artist consciously tends to identify two objects which have only some predicates in common. Regarding the nature of connectedness Hallman (1963) writes :

> "Logically the connectedness comprises relationship which are neither symmetrical nor transitive ; that is, newly created wholes are not equal to parts being connected . . . the relationship is neither inferential nor causal, it is metaphoric and transformational" (Gowan, et al. 1967, p. 19).

The second essential characteristic of creativity is that the product (idea, object, relationship etc.) should be original. Any product to be genuinely called original (and hence, creative), or to exist as idiographic, non-classifiable object, should contain four qualities : *novelty*, *uniqueness*, *unpredictability* and *surprise*.

Speaking psychologically, this condition refers to primary processes or the types of mental operations that are supposed to originate the idea. Even those who are not inclined psychoanalytically agree that certain 'unconscious mental operations' are at the heart of metaphoric function of the mind.

The process is 'non-rational' (as Hallman and others use the term) because the combinatorial activity manifests itself in the form of unconscious mental operations. It neither belongs to the rational mind, nor can it be consciously controlled. Non-rationality is not merely a condition of novelty, it is a cause. The psychoanalytic thinkers, notably Freud (1927, 1933), Jung (1946), Kris (1952), and Arieti (1976) are of this view.

According to Rogers (1961), 'Openness to Experience' includes four distinct sets of meanings, : *sensitivity, tolerance of ambiguity, self a ceptance* and *spontaneity.* Unlike other conditions, it refers not to the process or product, but to the potentially creative personality. These conditions also have some relevance for the "press" factors : the environmental conditions that exist external to the person. Stated differently, these sets of meanings refer to acquired traits of the potentially creative person.

To sum up, the concept of creativity lies in making associations that are remote, or unusual, or original in the sense of being statistically infrequent, unpredictable, novel, and unique. Such associations are not causally derivable. That the process is non-rational implies that certain unconscious or pre-conscious mental operations are at play in creative imagination.

Having thus realized the role of creativity in the enrichment of culture, and with broader conceptualization of giftedness, we cannot afford to anchor education to I.Q. based concept of giftedness. Fuller expression of the innate potentialities of the pupils is, of necessity, to be considered one of the important goals of education. But to successfully achieve the goal what is needed are identification, recognition and nurturance of the creatively gifted children. For all this what is desirable and essential is that parents and teachers should change their attitudes towards pupils who display such divergent behaviours ; and their idiosyncratic behaviour patterns should be psychologically understood.

Furthermore, for proper nurturance the curriculum framers, the teachers, and parents should not feel contented in merely accepting the cognitive and emotional divergence of behaviour, rather, should encourage the manifestation of such behaviours ;

only that can ensure fuller expression of the inherent powers of students. As a corollery to it, we need to allow the child more freedom in the classroom. The effective implementation of the programme of education for creativity also entails educating the parents and the teachers to enable them to realize the true meaning of cognitive development. In the school setting the methods of teaching and the evaluation procedures need a thorough change and a break away from what is banal and commonplace. In teaching-learning, for example, self exploration and discovery approach should guide the process ; in evaluation open ended questions and discussions should more frequently be used.

But the traditional teachers and most parents, it is afraid, will criticize such a programme. They may apprehend that so much freedom given to the child in the classroom or out side of it will jeopardize discipline, which consequently may adversely affect learning. But is not such fear ill-founded ? It is so ; because, such people conceive of discipline too narrowly. J. Krishnamurthi, the great Indian thinker in education, aptly remarks that true discipline does not lie in that students receive instructions (or exhortations) from the teachers silently and attentively ; instead, it lies in the "order" that springs from within—the result of internal harmony and integration. It is natural and spontaneous. It is discernible through commotion in the class room, resulting from self directed activities of children. The teachers role in the classroom is to provide intellectual climate in terms of thought-provoking situations to the growing minds. His role also lies in motivating them intrinsically ; only then the students will become autonomous, self-propelled thinkers.

This, no doubt, is a challenging task, especially in Indian conditions, where people are anchored to traditions and inhibitions of various sorts. But if we are to be counted as producers of knowledge (instead of being merely consumers of it) we are left with no alternative but to accept the challenge.

Creative and his Mental Health

Creativity may be described as an ineffable and sui-generis phenomenon : it is said to be a prerogative of man ; so is the person who creates. The creatively gifted individual diverges much from the intellectually gifted one, and also from rest of human population. He is known for his independence of thinking and non-conformity to group pressures, a sensitive temperament and introverted behaviour ; and is also characterized by autonomy of will. Such characterization of the creative personality is well established on both empirical and theoretical grounds. Torrance, MacKinnon, Barron, Guilford, Maslow, Rogers, Stein, Cattell, Arieti etc. have ascertained the presence of such factors in creative personality both empirically and theoretically. There is, however, another aspect of his personality which has remained controversial. Thinkers in the field have variously perceived and interpreted this facet of the life of a creative individual. The question, whether the creative individual is mentally healthy or emotionally deranged, still remains to be solved and decided unequivocally. Basing their arguments on historical and also on empirical evidence, different psychologists put divergent and sometimes, even, conflicting claims. Some of them tend to associate creativity with positive mental health ; yet there are others who claim a positive relationship of creativity with mental illness, and not with mental health. But before some appropriate design can be prepared to test the said relationship empirically, an intensive scanning of research literature is most needed. It is only then that one can peep into the psychodynamics of this intricate process—the uniquely human phenomenon, and some definite hypotheses can be framed and tested accordingly.

The Italian psychiatrist C. Lombroso (Arieti, 1976) strongly believes that positive relationship exists between genius and mental illness. In an article, *Genius and Insanity* (Lombroso, 1891), it was shown that a large number of geniuses suffered from neurological diseases ranging from neurosis to full-fledged psychosis. Lombroso's list includes Julius Caesar, Mohammad, Petrarch, Moliere, Napoleon, Dostovsky, Newton, Rousseau, and Schopenhaur who had occasional attacks of insanity. Among great musicians Mozart, Schumann, Beethovan, Donizethi, Hoffman, and Gluck suffered from frequent mental illness. Lombroso believed that genius may be an expression of 'degenerative psychosis' (Arieti 1976, pp. 354-355).

Jacobson (1926), on the other hand, holds that creative men may be of insane temperament, but this hinders their creativity. He further mentions that creative persons suffering from such mental sickness produce their best work in the healthiest period of their lives.

Lange Eichbaum (1932) stated that a large group of geniuses became psychotic but only when they had completed their great works. The list includes Baudelaire, Copernicus, Donizethi, Faraday, Kant, Newton, etc. But Eichbaum also admits that many creative geniuses did their work in the midst of their psychosis. Some of such creatives were Monet, Maupassant, and Rousseau. Their psychosis could not colour their work ; and the two remained distinct. Holderline and Van Gogh, nevertheless, were exception to this : their psychosis affected the content and form of their creative work. Eichbaum also includes in this list a large group of geniuses who were on the borderline of mental illness, but did not suffer from fullfledged psychotic disorders. In this group he includes Beethovan, Byron, Heine, Michelangelo and Schopenhaur. They possessed eccentric personalities, and were far from we normally connote a mentally healthy person. Pickering (1974), more recently, in his book, *Creative Malady*, describes creative malady of Darwin, F. Nightingale, Marry Baker Eddy, S. Freud, Marcel Proust, and Elizabeth Browning. According to him, Darwin and Nightingale suffered from psychoneurosis ; Nightingale, for sometime, was morphine addict. Eddy suffered from Hysteria due to her unresolved conflicts between her natural personality and what she wanted to project to the world. Pickering, referring to Jone's biography of Freud, states that Freud suffered from anxiety hysteria. Marcel Proust suffered from asthma. Elizabeth Barret was morphine addict (who later became Elizabeth Browning), and she remained so till her death.

Roth (1976) considers conflict as one of the two great motivating forces for original work, the other being the desire for self-expression immanent in us all. Arlow and Brenner (1964) are of the opinion that successful resolution of conflict may result in formation of permanent ego structures or functions which are stable in nature and whose mode of activity no longer reflects the impulsive nature of the original drive component. Thus, they favour the presence of conflict as a drive for novel work.

Apart from evidence based on biographical studies in the context of creativity and mental illness, psychoanalytic view also asserts that conflict and other neurotic tendencies lie at the root of originality and some other form of creative self-expression. Bellak (1958) holds that the quantity of 'Ego regression' is displayed both by those who are creative and those who are mentally disturbed, although the former manage to synthesize, and thus are able to increase their adaptive capacities.

May (1959), on the other hand, while criticizing the Freudian view of Creativity, holds just the opposite viewpoint. He points out that such a reducing of creative activity to neurotic process is not proper ; and asserts that creativity is related to mental health and not to disease or neurosis.

Some of the contemporary investigators of May, including Maslow (1959, 1962), Rogers (1959), and Fromm (1959) join hands with what May (1959) has claimed. They tend to prove that creativity can occur in well adjusted individuals only. To Maslow, for example, "creative expression, in some form, is an endeavour to self-actualization. It is a process of 'realizing and completing oneself by an integration within, and between self and the world. It is through this process that "self becomes unified, more open to experience, and more fully-functioning" (Taylor, 1975).

Barron (Gowan et al. 1967) argues somewhat differently. According to him, the imbalance in creative personality is only apparent: the fact remains that they are healthier than the average. The cause of the apparent imbalance, according to Barron, is the gap that occurs between the creative and the social majority. He describes the creative individual as a person who is sensitive, possesses a high energy level, and ability for complex synthesis.

Interestingly enough, Torrance (1964) too empirically found that the creative person is extremely sensitive and requires independence. In an earlier article, Torrance (1961, pp. 31-34) tries to give somewhat convincing reasons why a creative individual is apt to be involved in problems. He writes: "Inescapably, the individual who thinks of a new idea is in the very beginning a minority of one . . . there are very few people who can tolerate being a minority of one, since, creativity involves independence of mind, non-conformity to group pressures or breaking out of the mould, it is inevitable that highly creative children experience some unusual problems." Thus, the highly creative child either must repress his creativity or learn to cope with tensions which arise from being a minority of one. Repression of creative needs may lead to actual personality break-down. Their expression frequently leads to loneliness, conflicts, and other problems of adjustment.

Resume

A scanning of the above mentioned (divergent, yet convincing) arguments may lead one to the conclusion that the life of a creative individual is not a smooth sailing. He seems to be confronted by problems of various sorts, viz., social, emotional, of adjustment etc. Nevertheless, what marks him uniquely is that he is a highly motivated individual, endeavouring towards self-actualization of what potentially he 'is.' Ensuing of anxiety in the life of such a person, therefore, seems natural.

The same may be substantiated by the fact of his heightened sensitivity to environment—both physical and social, and his easy access to primary processes (regression in the service of Ego). Zukerman and Spielberger (1976, p. 123) quote Averill according to whom potentiality for anxiety is inherent in man nature who lives in a largely symbolic universe of his own construction. Anxiety is not merely a sign of pathology, it is a part of (creative) human potential. The fact that the lives of many of the great geniuses have been full of turmoil and turbulance, and of conflicts—particularly relating to cognitive ambiguities—does at least suggest that anxiety (or more correctly anxiety-proneness) and creativity in an individual go together. The queerness and eccentricity of attitudes become part and parcel of the life style of such geniuses. The investigator, therefore, hypothesizes that potential for creativity and anxiety proneness occur concomitantly. But the question that still remains unanswered is, "Do the two campus—the one associating creativity with positive mental health, and the other depicting the life of great creative genius as full of conflicts, and in some cases, leading to psychopathology—contradict each other ?

This investigator opines that the contradiction is, in fact, not real. The two groups view the problem from two different angles. There seems no doubt in the fact that a potentially high creative individual perceives incompleteness, void or, at least, cognitive gaps between parts of the same reality. He, therefore, directs his energies in bridging the gap through his unique interpretation of reality. This perceived gap may be hypothesized as the source of anxiety in such an individual. But when he is able to fill up the gap, he feels delighted. Thus, with every creative achievement he adds to his growth and development. Creativity, therefore, may be an endeavour on the part of creative individual to alleviate anxiety which was occasioned by his perceptualized cognitive gap

Such a hypothesis can perhaps be better understood in the light of what McReynolds (1976) holds as cause of anxiety.

According to McReynolds the sole cause of anxiety is congnitive backlog created as a result of unassimilated "percepts" in the cognitive structures of the individual. Evidently, such unassimilation of "percepts" causes some confusion and turbulance in the mind of the potentially creative child which ensues anxiety in him. In his effort to assimilate the unassimilated content (by creating unique relationships) he is both alleviating that particular instance of anxiety, and simultaneously stepping towards growth which Maslow would call 'self-actualization.' But again a potentially creative person would perceive such cognitive incongruencies, and hence feel anxious till such perceptual incongruencies are removed. So the moments of anxiety and moments of delight occur simultaneously. It may, however, be well understood that the intent of investigator is not to prove any cause-effect relationship ; neither he wants to say that occurrence of anxiety is conducive to creative growth. He simply wants to hypothesize that potentially creative person is anxiety-prone (because he can see incongruencies and "gaps of knowledge" more quickly than others). If he is not given the facilitating climate for his self-expression, or if he fails to create such an environment, he may be over-whelmed by anxiety which ultimately may take a pathological form.

With the ultimate goal of helping a potentially creative child actualize his latent talents we must empirically see the role of anxiety or anxiety-proneness in shaping his personality. It was in view of the above theoretical background that the investigator chose to find out the relationship between anxiety and creative thinking in the context of certain dimensions of personality. Now what is required is the precise statements of the hypotheses concerning the problem. Before this job can successfully be done, a systematic treatment of various theories of creativity, the nature and cause of anxiety, and a mention of the dimensions of human personality is most needed. The next chapter, therefore, is designed to delineate these concepts so that the study can be pursued scientifically in directions warranted by the above background.

CHAPTER II

Theoretical Orientation of the Problem

With a view to understand the problem as stated in the previous chapter in general, and to reach certain definite, tenable hypotheses for empirical verification, in particular, it is necessary to explore its theoretical background. The theoretical framework that follows, primarily focuses on three things : (i) a critical review of the theories of creativity, (ii) Meaning of anxiety, and (iii) a brief outline of the structure of human personality. The personological considerations seem to inevitably enter into any such investigation related to behavioural sciences. It is, perhaps, a common observation that innate dispositions, the psychological and biological factors of human personality significantly determine how an individual is going to react to certain conditions that are situation-specific. And secondly, the rationale for including personality variables in an investigation of this type seem to be obvious owing arguments as given by Barron (1956) in this context. Barron says, "original responses occur with regularity among some persons while among others original responses are virtually non-existent." He further adds that "studies using known groups of adults, that is, groups of adults who are generally engaged in performance of tasks that are judged to be creative in nature, as opposed to groups of adults not generally engaged in performance of such tasks, have reported general agreement in terms of a personality traits that are important to these sort of tasks."

With these considerations in view, the investigator has attempted a critical review of the variables on which the present investigation is based.

Theories of Creativity—A Critical Review

From the foregoing discussion of the concept of creativity, it is probably easy to infer that the concept is elusive ; elusive in the sense that it is and can be conceptualized in different perspectives depending upon the viewpoint(s) from which one looks at the phenomenon. It is for this reason that to define creativity in such a way as to include all viewpoints, seems difficult, if not impossible at present. A study of the pertinent literature on the subject of creativity supports the conclusion that there are certain definite approaches/theories to make the concept explicit. Taylor (1975) differentiates between the various levels at which an individual may be creative. He distinguishes five levels of creativity in an ascending hierarchy. The first level, *expressive creativity*, involves independent expression where skills, originality and quality of the product are not very important. This is exemplified in the spontaneous drawings of children. Taylor notes that creative experiences at this level are pre-requisites to later, more advanced and more highly controlled creative achievement.

The second level—*productive creativity*—is distinguished by the facts that at this level the individual gains mastery over some portion of the environment, and produces something. The object produced need not be distinguishable from the products of others. *Inventive creativity* which constitutes the third level, is marked by the presence of ingenuity. The new uses of old parts, as exemplified in the accomplishments of inventors, explorers, and discoverers, who seek new ways of old things are handy instances of "inventive creativity."

Those who make significant alterations in the basic foundations or principles of a theory, have achieved the fourth level which Taylor names *innovative creativity.* Innovative creativity is based upon highly developed abstract conceptualizing skills.

Emergentive creativity—the fifth and the highest level—is a rare occurrence. It requires ability to absorb experiences which are commonly provided, and to produce therefrom something that is unique. The formulations of Einstein, Freud, Picasso, Wright, Tulsi Dass, Ramanujan, Tagore, etc. may be cited as representative examples of creativity at this level.

Arieti (1976), following a different approach, still over simplifies such categorization of creativity theories and puts all such theories only in two categories. The first category is related to those ideas or theories which attempt to deal with the subject from the point of view of creativity as a process and describing the different phases or stages that can be observed in the event of emergence of some creative product.

The second category theories, according to Arieti, are those which attempt to explain not the observable symptoms, but rather the hypothesized mental mechanisms that can explain the occurrence of creative thinking. The first category which he calls the *general psychological,* is perhaps an attempt to answer, what happens/occurs when . . . ? The second category, which he calls the *psychoanalytic,* is probably an attempt to answer the question, whatever that occurs/happens, how and why does it occur/happen ?

A brief outline of the two categories is attempted below. From the point of view of the present investigation both of these categories are important, as they shed light on the nature of creativity in different perspectives.

General Psychological Conceptualisation Regarding Creativity

The attempt that considers creativity as a process, occurring in time, and describing the various phases or stages, can historically, be traced from Wallas (1926). Wallas, in his book entitled, "*The Art of Thought*", discussed four distinct phases of the creative process. These four phases are ; Preparation, Incubation, Illumination, and Verification. At the 'preparation' stage the individual is free to think, to collect information, to listen, or to do various kinds of inquiring activities. During 'incubation,' the information unconsciously undergoes certain changes or modifications. That is, incubation is a period of rest for the conscious mental activities. Then comes the third and the real stage—illumination—which yields the creative solution to the problem which the conscious mind could not find. It is a sort of intuition or clear insight—something that lies between a hunch and a solution. At the fourth stage i.e. 'verification' one works upon the idea, and gives it the form of a finished creative product. This happens quite often, with many of us in routine life. One thinks about a problem for its solution ; tries hard, but fails. Then one goes to bed ; but sometimes, when he awakes, he awakes with a solution. The discovery of Fuschian functions by Poincare in mathematics, and Archemedes principle in Physics are clear illustrations of this process.

Rossman (1931) examined the creative process and found that the process occurs not in four stages but in seven, which are as follows :

(i) Observation of a need or a difficulty.

(ii) Analysis of the need.

(iii) Survey of all the available information.

(iv) Formulation of all the objective solutions.

(v) Critical analysis of these solutions.

(vi) Birth of a new idea—the invention.

(vii) Experimentation to test the most promising solution ; and selection and perfection of the final embodiment by some or all of the previous steps.

Osborn (1953) used slightly different terminology and gave the following seven stages.

(i) *Orientation* - pointing to the problem.

(ii) *Preparation* - gathering pertinent data.

(iii) *Analysis* - breaking down the relevant material.

(iv) *Ideation*—piling up alternatives by ways of ideas.

(v) *Incubation*—'letting up', to invite illumination.

(vi) *Synthesis*—putting up the pieces together to prepare a whole.

(vii) *Evaluation*—judging the result.

More recently, Stein (1974) divided the creative process in three stages only. These are : (i) Stage of Hypothesis Formation, (ii) Stage of Hypothesis testing, (iii) Stage of Communicating the Results. However, he points out that 'preparation' or 'education' precedes these stages.

Wertheimer (1945), the Gestaltian, explains the phenomenon of creativity as a process moving from a structurally unstable or unsatisfactory situation (S_1) to a situation (S_2) which is structurally stable. According to him, grouping, organization, and structuralization occur in all thinking that is creative. There is another mechanism often followed in such types of thinking. The individual envisions some features of S_2 and from these the creative person captures the whole.

Arthur Koestler, though not a psychologist, tried to explain the phenomenon in his works, *The Act of Creation* (1949) and *Insight and Outlook* (1964) with the help of a fundamental concept that he calls '*bisociation*'. Bisociation, according to him, is any mental event or occurrence simultaneously associated with two habitually incompatible contexts

Guilford (1959) discusses the concept of creativity as a cognitive ability, multivariate in nature. He, following a factor analytic approach, brings out the components that constitute creative thinking. He names such cognitions as divergent productions which are *Flexibilily, Originality, Fluency,* and *Elaboration.* A reference to his Structure of Intellect Model has already been made.

Guilford, indeed, is not concerned with creative process as it occurs in time and stages ; instead, he analyses the nature of creative thinking ability, which he equates with divergent thinking. These components of divergent thinking constitute the 'potential', which may unfold in a suitable climate. It is a type of thinking that does not follow the beaten path of conformity and convention but proceeds towards unusual solutions to the problem. Guilfords' concept is, thus, useful from the point of view of assessment of this unique ability in children.

The attempts made by the psychologists mentioned above are worthwhile and cannot be ignored ; but when viewed from another point of view, with the possible exception of Wertheimer and Koestler, "The Psychological approaches—commendable as they are, as pioneering approaches—have only scratched the surface of a complicated psychological phenomenon. Such concepts as illumination, divergency, fluency, and so forth do not take us very far ...they refer to end-products at conscious level, the outcome of many previous conscious or pre-conscious mechanisms. These terms correspond to what in psychiatry, is called 'Manifest Symptomology ... A good psychiatrist wants to go further. As much as he can, he must try to understand the mechanisms that brought about the symptoms, the meaning of the context of symptoms, and why the symptoms have assumed that particular form" (Arieti 1976 p. 20). Such theories, in fact, do not indicate what may be called the psychodynamics of the creative process. In order to have a deeper insight into psychodynamics of the process, therefore, an over view of psychoanalytic theories becomes essential.

Psychoanalyst's Views of Creativity

Freud, the father of psychoanalysis and 'depth psychology' made the first attempt to understand the intricate process of creativity. The theory is furthered by Kris (1952), Kubie (1958), Greenacre (1957), Weissman (1958), Jung (1957), and Arieti (1967, 1976). These Thinkers seem to make a break through to reach the configuration—the innermost psychological mechanisms. It is these theories which tend to answer the basic question—'how does it occur ?' From the perusal of the psychological theories given above it appears that there is a total absence of psychological arousal in a creative act. But these is sufficient evidence in the history of thought, literature, art, and science that clearly proves the presence of such arousal, at least, in the form of cognitive gaps. Perceptualization of such incongruencies/gaps in the cognitive structure leads to engendering of anxiety or arousal' in some form. Though historical evidence does not necessarily entail the existence of association/relationship between creativity and emotionality, it does, however, show that most creative geniuses have been crazy or queer sort of persons. Such fringes of thought have found sustenance under the umbrella of cognitive or emotional conflict and the historical evidence in this regard does suggest that in a scientific study of creativity and the creative person, such factors as emotionality, anxiety etc. cannot be ignored. Freud too affirms the importance of unconscious processes, especially of unconscious motivation. Freud (1908) visualized a similarity between neurosis and creative thinking. According to him both originate in conflict, especially in that which basically springs from fundamental biological drives. The concept of '*sublimation*', according to Freud, plays a significant role in creativity, which according to him is a diversion of libidinal energy in socially desirable and personally gratifying ways.

It appears from Freud's analysis that he attached execssive importance to the process of motivation in human personality in the context of creativity. But such reduction of the whole phenomenon to motivational mechanisms seems unjust. In this context Arieti (1976) remarks, "Practically all human behaviour is motivated but only a small part of it can be called creative. There is no reason why we cannot assume that, in some cases, creative attempts are made for the purpose of correcting an unsatisfying reality. But is reality unsatisfying because of sexual frustration or neurosis alone ? Is the creative person's discontents only a disguise for lack of sexual gratification ? What about his discontent in other aspects of the human predicament ? The crucial problem is to determine why and how a few gifted men are able to transform their motivations and the effects of their early or late personal experiences into creative product. Important as it may be to discover why certain peoples have the need to create. It is far more important to find out how this need is transformed into spiritual vision or an epoch-making discovery" (p. 23).

Binswanger (1976, p. 57), the existentialist thinker, poses some very pertinent questions for psychoanalysis in his discussion of creativity. He says, "Is suffering necessarily a sign of abnormality and if not, when not ? Is guilt always pathological ? Is maladjustment to social demands (always) a symptom of emotional disorder ?"

Among those who worked within the theoretical framework of Freud, Kris (1952) is, perhaps, the most important. To Kris, creativity is a 'regression in the service of the Ego.'

The regression in the service of Ego makes use of primary process (the concept of primary and secondary processes was given by Freud in his, 'The Analysis of Dreams', 1901). What seems to be unclear is whether primary process is really a manifestation of regression or is it simply 'an emerging' 'accessibility or availability' which is connected with regression only occasionally ?

The second difficulty with Kris is that he could not move out of the libidinal framework of Freud. He believes in system preconscious in creativity.

The other psychoanalyst Kubie (1958), for example, supports Kris's idea regarding the use of preconscious and not of unconscious mental mechanisms in the creative act. It is here that they differ with Freud. According to Kubie both conscious and unconscious mental activities hinder creative activity ; the latter because of the 'rigid use of symbolic functions' while the former, with its 'anchorage to reality'. Both Kubie and Kris emphasize the use of preconscious mental activities in creative acts.

Greenacre (1957) is yet another thinker who worked within the Freudian framework. Pointing out to the 'dissociative' function of the ego, he remarks that the ego in the creative act dissociates itself from the real objects and develops a 'love affair with the world'. As regards the personality traits of the creative person, Greenacre holds that such a child shows more sensitivity to sensory stimulation than the average child. It is this excessive sensory stimulation that helps him intensify and also broaden the experience.

Influenced by Greenacre, Weissman (1967) believed that because of the intensified sensory stimulation the creative infants even hallucinate real objects. He, thus, substituted Kris's concept of 'regression' in the service of the Ego by 'dissociative functions' of the Ego. While using dissociative function, the creative child may partially 'decathect' the external object and 'hyper-cathect' the imaginative perception of it.

Jung is another very important theorist whose contribution to creativity is quite substantial. According to Phillipson (1963)

Jung viewed creativity at two levels : (a) the psychological mode, in which the content is derived from the realm of human consciousness, in relation to such things as love, family environment, society, crime and the like. But in such a mode creativity nowhere transcends the bounds of psychological intelligibility ; (b) the visionary mode of creativity wherein the content is derived not from the life experiences but from the timeless depth, which Jung called the 'collective unconscious'. The collective unconscious of Jung is the repository of the primordial experience (the archetypes) accumulated in the course of generations. It is because of this reason, perhaps, that archetypes, sometimes, surpass even man's understanding.

The visionary mode in creativity, according to Jung, is not subject to conscious control of the individual. Sometimes, such a person feels an 'alien will' beyond his comprehension. In Jung's theory animation of the collective unconscious, the archetypes, explains the causation of the process of creativity. It might be for this reason that the great work of art transcends the life experiences, personal factors, and historical periods in which such an individual happens to live. Somehow, the re-awakening of the hidden treasures of experience, dormant in collective unconscious, takes place. In the event of emergence of such creativity the individual is unable to adapt to reality. This inability to adapt to reality, instead of being a hurdle, facilitates him to re-awaken that which is hidden deep into unconscious, and further induces him to enter into 'mystical participation' with the ancient and the obsolete.

Arieti (1976) draws much upon deep psychology propounded by Freud, yet his differences with the father of psychoanalysis are also obvious. In divulging the concept, Arieti is not much concerned with the surface definition of the creative product ; he is more interested in the mental mechanisms that explain creativity in the artistic field as well as in the field of pure sciences and mathematics.

Second, Arieti's exposition of creativity seems quite interesting, in that, he draws similarity between creativity and mental illness (schizophrenia, in particular), while at the same time maintains a clear difference between the two.

To begin with, Arieti (1974, 1976,) considers creativity and mental illness as two transformations of reality. Both the creative and the psychotic want to transform the world. The creative person wants to change reality in order to beautify it, or to change the field of human knowledge and experience in order to provide usefulness, understanding, predictability, and evoke a universal response. The psychotic, instead, wants to transform reality in a way that fits his private way of feeling, his delusional thinking ; and does so in ways which do not evoke consensus but often remain strictly individualistic, bizarre strange, incommunicable, and even destructive to the self and to others.

Arieti criticizes both Lombroso's view as well as Freud's. He says that if psychiatry made the first mistake about creativity with Cesare Lombroso, it made second one with Freud's idea that the whole process could be explained in terms of early conflicts and unconscious motivation. Lombroso, first of all, had inferred that creative person and mentally ill person had something in common psychologically, but somhow he was not able to point out what it was. He made the mistake of concluding that a creative person is mentally ill, probably, epileptic.

Freud (1901), in his book, *The Interpretation of Dreams* conceived of operations of the mind consisting of two modalities, the primary process and the secondary process. Drawing largely from formulations of Freud, Arieti interprets creative process as a '*magic synthesis*' of these two modalities, and names it the "tertiary process."

Freud had maintained that the primary process

originates in the primitive part of the mind, called the 'Id' and archaic 'Ego'. In its pure form the process is generally followed in dreams, pathological conditions, and in childhood, before the secondary process is developed. In the normal course of our life, or in our daily contact with reality, we generally follow the secondary process—called the logical thinking. There is no doubt that the onset of secondary process also is made in the childhood but its development takes time. The primary process re-appears in the creative process also, bringing with it content that consists of obsolete, ancient and primitive mental mechanisms, generally relegated to the recesses of the psyche. But, the reappearance of the primary process in creative work is in "strange, intricate combinations" with the secondary process mechanisms. It is from approprite and unpredictable matching with the secondary process that the primitive forms of cognitions, generally confined to abnormal conditions, become innovative powers. The tertiary process, with specific mechanisms of forms, blends the two works of mind and matter, and in many cases, rational with the irrational ; instead of rejecting the primitive the creative mind intergrates it with the normal psychological processes. It is from this synthesis, called by Arieti - 'the magic synthesis'—that the new, the unexpected and the desirable emerge (Arieti, 1976).

The first way in which the primary process operates, both in a schizophrenic and a creative person is 'identity based on similarity'. A schizophrenic, on the basis of similarity of some predicates between two objects, identifies them. In this process of identifying, the schizophrenic is not conscious of the duality and distinctness of the two, rather, takes them as the same. It is just like that a child calls every picture of a female as mummy and that of male as daddy. This phenomenon can be explained in Freudian terms as 'complete regression to the womb'. Arieti calls it 'the sole use of primary process thinking.' This primary process thinking is also found at the base of cultural repertorie, foundations of many societal or collective manifestations—rituals, customs, beliefs, etc. The same paleologic thinking or primary process thinking also occurs in the works of a large majority of creative persons. Similes and metaphors are formed through sharing of predicates, though, not logically acceptable yet they have aesthetic values. Through symbolic use of language, paleologic thinking increases the power of imagination or imagery ; imagination, more accurately, is a precusor of creativity—a springboard to it.

The difference between the use of primary process thinking by a shizophrenic and a creative artist lies probably in the fact, that a creative person consciously uses primary process so as to lend beauty to his expression, while a schizophrenic suffers from what Arieti calls 'Adualism' i.e. he is not conscious that the two realities are distinct and separate.

This emergence of the tertiary class is not what Reichenback (1951) called the induction by enumeration ; instead it is a case of, what some authors have called, induction by intuition. Frank (1957) calls it induction by imagination. Arieti calls it induction by creativity. Creativity, in such instances, consists in (i) individualizing a common property, (ii) not identifying the objects having some such properties with primary classes, (iii) recognizing that they belong to unsuspected secondary class (such as gravitational bodies). When such a new class is discovered it leads to the discovery of new properties hidden in the member of this class. Formation of new concepts is also based upon such a principle of similarity of predicates.

Another primary process mechanism, common to dreams and schizophrenia on the one hand, and the creatives on the other, is the 'concretization and perceptualization' of an abstract concept. According to Arieti (1974), in schizophrenia, concepts that cannot be endured by patients at an abstract level, are translated into concrete representations. The concepts becomes specific and concrete, the indefinite feelings become finite, the imperceptible becomes perceptible. In the case of a patient, the vague menace is transformed into a specific threat. It is no longer the whole horrible world that is against the patient, rather, "they" in particular, are against him.

One can, on the other hand, easily visualize that such concretizations are abundantly found in the work of a fine artist or a poet, where the abstract concepts are transformed into perceptible images (Goddess Saraswati, for example). The difference between psychopathologic use of primary process and that of an artist lies in 'no consciousness', or 'consciousness' respectively of abstraction. In the case of a schizophrenic, the power of abstraction, in fact, is completely impaired, and the patient follows only the concrete channels. Whereas in the case of artist, the use of primary process does not eliminate the abstract ; on the contrary, it is through the medium of primary process that the abstract concept emerges. The schizophrenic uses it as a psychological defence ; the creative person uses it for aesthetic and scientific purposes. For the one, there is constriction of personality, for the other, an expansion of it. Arieti quotes Andre-Breton, the poet psychiatrist, who put it that the creative image lends to the abstract the mask of the concrete.

Meaning of Anxiety

Anxiety enters into man's life with the first breath and ends with the last. This proposition may be true for most human beings. Anxiety, in a way, is the most intimate experience to man : almost co-existent with life ; yet the most ineffable phenomenon. In order to theorize anxiety, one may direct one's thinking towards seeking answer to two simple question. First, what is the nature of the experience of anxiety ? That is, how does it affect the human organism, or what are the felt aspects of it ; and second, what are the situations or conditions existing in the environment or in the organism or in both, under which the said experience happens to occur ? What is attempted below is an effort to seek answer to these two questions with a view to arrive at a clear interpretation of anxiety.

While, on the one hand, anxiety is described as the hub of all mental disorders (Freud), on the other, it is said to be associated with the subtlest of human thought. One may be reminded of Jai Shankar Prasad's *Kamayani,* wherein he describes anxiety as an acutely distressing human experience, yet generative of most creative expression of human personality. Similarly associating anxiety with positive mental health, Arieti (1976) quotes a number of studies including those of Lombroso, Jacobson, Eichbaum, Roth, and Pickering which indicate the possibility of an association between mental health and creativity.

A number of existentialist thinkers too, including Tillich, Neibuhr, Kierkegaard etc., talk of anxiety as a force responsible for human growth and development (cf. Rollo May, 1950). Even psychoanalysts like Erich Fromm and Goldstein associate anxiety with transforming powers. According to Tillich, anxiety is a "reaction to threat of non-being" or meaninglessness aiming at activizing the self to save itself from dissolution and making it "distinct from the world of non-beings-of objects." Neibuhr posits the source of man's anxiety due to his position in the world vis-a-vis his freedom. According to him, "man being both bound and free, both limited and limitless, is anxious. Anxiety is an inevitable paradox of freedom and finiteness in which man is involved" (Rollo May, 1950, 12-13).

Similarly Kierkegaard's conception of anxiety is a natural outcome of the central thesis of existentialism—the ontological freedom of man. According to him, self-actualization or individuation is the goal of human life. In the process of individuation man is faced with 'possibility' and 'choice.' As the child grows it develops self awareness that leads him to choose between alternatives, and brings him in confrontation with his environment. The problem, thus, concerns inner conflict which results in anxiety. Beneath all this lies the ontological freedom of man ; for, if man would not free he could not be held responsible for choice, and conflict would not and could not occur. So Kierkegaard appears right in holding that anxiety is inherent in man's freedom, choice and responsibility (1944, 131-140).

In order to get an insight into the true nature of anxiety let us first scan the available psychological literature on the subject starting with Freud to the present time.

Freud's view of Anxiety

According to Freud (1959, XX 1337) Anxiety "is a special state of unpleasure with acts of discharge along particular paths." Differentiating anxiety with fear he describes three types of anxiety : Reality Anxiety, Moral Axiety, and Neurotic Anxiety. Reality anxiety is essentially synonymous with fear, and can be stated as a painful emotional experience caused due to dangerous situation of the organism. This kind of anxiety is learned through simple learning processes related to or acquired from early experience of helplessness. Moral anxiety is the experience of guilt or shame, and results from the perception of danger from the Super-ego. To begin with, it is a fear of being punished by parents. Neurotic anxiety is caused by perception of danger from Id-instincts i.e., the danger feared in neurotic anxiety is simply that of inner instinctual limpulses : it is a fear about what would happen should one fail to attain what one intends to attain.

Commenting on Freud's view of anxiety, Fischer (1970) writes that according to Freud, Ego is the actual seat of anxiety. It is responsible for maintaining accurate relations with the environment, a break down in the Ego functions would certainly disrupt one's relations with external reality. During anxiety the Ego perceives a danger situation. The danger may have its source in the external world (*reality anxiety*), or in the Super-ego (*moral anxiety*), or in the Id (*neurotic anxiety*).

Unlike Freud, some psychologists do not qualitatively differentiate different forms of anxiety ; instead, they consider different forms of anxiety as quantitative divergence from normal idiosyncracies. Distinguishing neurotic anxiety from normal anxiety, May (1950, 197) maintains that neurotic anxiety is a reaction which (i) is disproportionate to objective threat, (ii) involves repression or other mechanisms of intra-psychic conflicts, and (iii) requires neurotic defence mehanisms for its management.

Neo-Freudian Approaches

The basic difference between Freudian and Neo-Freudian approaches to the concept of anxiety lies in their conception of man. For Freud, man is nothing more than an animal struggling for survival. His is purely a mechanistic view. On the other hand, the Neo-Freudians place due emphasis on social matrix without which man's existence may be impossible. The view of some of the major Neo-Freudians e.g. Sullivan, Jacobson, Schachtel etc. are reviewed in brief here to highlight their basic premises.

For Sullivan, man's existence is inconceivable without the existence of "other persons" with whom one is to have a dialogue in the form of interpersonal relations. Culture does not merely cause repression, but facilitates self-expression too. Man and society are thus seen as co-defining. Man, starting from infancy to adulthood, continually unfolds inter-personal relations with the "significant others". Anxiety, according to Sullivan, arises solely from the dysfunctions in the inter-personal relations of the individual with significant others. All tensions do not produce anxiety. For example, tension associated with satisfaction of bodily needs does not produce anxiety but tension that is associated with inter-personal relations invariably causes anxiety.

Anxiety, according to Sullivan, may be mild or severe, depending upon the real or fancied degree of significance of others, and the severity with which diapproval is communicated. The index of anxiety is a multiplicative of these two factors. The way is which anxiety is induced in most cases is what Sullivan terms "empathy". 'Empathy', here, refers to seeing oneself as others see him.

Sullivan's distinction of anxiety and fear is quite important. According to Sullivan, "fear...is a very widely distributed device of living organisms for the purpose of self-preservation. It is not exclusively human as anxiety is". (Sullivan, 1956, 91-92). Elsewhere he states : "fear, from the mildest to the most felt aspect of tension, arises from danger to the existence or biological integrity of the organism" (Sullivan 1953, 50). Anxiety unlike fear, is not adaptive.

Jacobson's Views

Freud over-emphasised Id processes—the instinctual gratification which he termed the pleasure principle. In Freudian psychology Ego and Super-ego have derived status. The role of Ego is as a mediator between the Id and the external reality whereas according to Ego-psychology it is fully autonomous, and acts as co-ordinator instead of mediator.

Freud had maintained a minimal level of excitation as a condition to homeostatic equilibrium, Jacobson, on the other hand, articulated that for the homeostatic process a medium optimal level of excitation is necessary. According to Freud's pleasure principle, any increase in tension requires immediate discharge regardless of consequences. Jacobson postulated, instead, that organism prefers certain paths for discharge of energy to gain pleasure. Accordingly, pleasure is not simply tension-reduction, it involves individual's preferences for particular tension discharge patterns. Therefore, pleasure principle, according to Jacobson, is a general tendency of the organism to maintain a medium optimal level of excitation through the use of preferred pathways of discharge.

Jacobson further argues that all affects (tensions) are not necessarily disruptive or unpleasant. Many affects are associated with normal Ego functioning and their tensional qualities do no not make them pleasant or unpleasant. She divides all affects into two categories :

1. Intro-systemic, i.e., those arising directly from the tension in the Id (sex, excitation, rage etc.), or tension in the Ego (healthy fear, pain, objects of love, and hate).

2. Inter-systemic i.e. those induced by tensions between (a) Ego and Id (viz. fear of Id, anxiety, complexes of disguest, shame and pity, (b) Ego and Super-ego (viz., guilt feeling depression etc.).

So, anxiety is a specific-state of unpleasure induced by inter-systemic tension (those between Ego and Id). In general anxiety communicates an impending state of danger to the Ego. It occurs when there is a blockage of tensional discharge through preferred pathways. Thus, Jacobson considers anxiety, primarily, as adaptive phenomenon that the Ego utilizes in continuing development and differentiation. While anxiety is a danger to the Ego, it also provides opportunity for the development of new and more appropriate discharge pathways i.e. behaviours.

Ernest Schachtel's Views

Schachtel is a psychoanalytic thinker. While admitting his indebtedness to Freud, he differs significantly from him. He believes that "man lives throughout his life in a conflict which Freud at one time described as that between *Eros* the unification principle, and *Thanatos*—the death principle, and which I would describe as the conflict of emergence from embeddedness." (Schachtel, 1959, 6). The principle of emergence refers to individual's interests in and inclination towards an ever expanding, stimulating world. The principle of embeddedness, on the other hand, refers to individual's needs for safety and security. So conflict lies in individual's needs to realize his potentialities while at the same time preserving his saftety, familiarity and at-homeness with both himself and his environment. To quote his statement,

> "Anxiety arises with any separation from the state of embeddedness or with the threat of such separation. . . The attempt to emerge from embeddedness (without any attempt for relatedness to higher level of development or of greater differentiation) sets off anxiety and some kind of helplessness is experienced by the individual in encountering the world. . . The area in which the threat of separation is most readily experienced, the extent of these areas and kinds of events or situations which are most likely to constitute such a threat, differ from one person to another in accordance with their life histories and probably also with the in-born predispositions towards anxiety" (1959, 44-45).

Otto Rank and K. Horney on Anxiety

Sharing Sahachtel's views Otto Rank relates anxiety to the central problem of human development, viz., individuation—the need to live as an autonomous individual. Anxiety, for him, is apprehension involved in separation. In the process of individuation one faces two forms of fears—the life fear and the death fear. The life fear is anxiety at going forward and becoming an individual. This is the apprehension involved in every new possibility of an autonomous activity. The death fear in anxiety is at going backward—losing individuality. A neurotic is one who is unable to manage these two forms of anxiety.

For K. Horney anxiety is a threat to what she called the "core or essence" of personality. It is a reaction to threat to what the individual holds essential to his existence as personality. According to Horney, individual develops some pattern as the basis of one's safety. Any thing which is likely to jeopardize the individual's specific protective pursuits may provoke anxiety. Horney distinguishes between fear and anxiety : fear is a reaction to specific danger to which specific adjustment at least in theory can be made, while anxiety is characterized by diffuseness and uncertainty.

Socio-Cultural Approach of Erich Fromm

E. Fromm, like Kierkegaard and Rank, views anxiety in the context of individual freedom and isolation. A child begins his life with primary ties with parents. During the process of growth he tends to be free from parental dependency and acquires individuation. The process of individuation involves some actual or potential threats. According to Fromm, this separation from a world which, in comparison wtih one's individual existence, is overwhelmingly strong and powerful, and often threatening and dangerous, creates a feeling of powerlessness and anxiety. As long as one was an integral part of the world, unaware of the possibilities and responsibilities of the individual action, one need not be afraid of it.

Fromm further holds that the nature of freedom is dialectical which operates at every step of human development. There are two possibilities : either one accepts to confront anxiety with the view to overcome it, or, one tries to allay it. The first possibility occurs in case one, while separating the ties (to acquire freedom), is ready for new relatedness, for new constellations. Such a state of affairs leads one to healthy and happy growth and development. The second possibility (of allaying anxiety) can also be dichotomized : the individual either accepts complete conformity to social demands (thereby surrendering his freedom and becoming an automaton) or tends to develop new dependencies, making compromises with anxiety-producing situation. In any of these ways the escape from anxiety is only temporary. The individual eventually comes under the grip of neurotic patterns of, what Arieti (1976) would call, "adjustment syndrome"—adjustment mechanism that apparently leads to adaptation to circumstances but ultimately may take a severe pathological form. The achievement of goals, in fact, is possible only through confronting anxiety and overcoming it.

Rollo May (1950) agrees largely with K. Horney and describes anxiety as a threat to the "core" or essence of personality—the security base of a person, or the values held essential by an individual to live as an integrated personality. Differentiating anxiety from fear, May holds that anxiety response is undifferentiated while the fear response is differentiated. What is threatened in anxiety experience is the security base which cannot be specifically located.

Cognitivists' View of Anxiety

Recently, McReyonlds (1976) gives somewhat altered meaning to the concept of anxiety. He mentions two types of anxiety—primary and secondary. Both differ in meaning and source.

Primary anxiety is caused as a result of "cognitive backlog". It is a function of this backlog (U). Mathematically primary anxiety is = fU. In explaining the term cognitive backlog, McReynolds assumes that (i) Incongruences in perception yield a conscious aversive feeling of tension. Such instances, if accumulated, cause what he calls, unassimilated percepts or cognitive backlog (U). The increment in cognitive backlog may be due to (a) occurrence or recurrence of unassimilated percepts, (b) input, at a rate more rapid than it can be assimilated, (c) de-assimilation of previously assimilated material. One may not, however, fully agree with such a theory, for, cognitive backlog as such (i.e. abrupt rise in U) may, at occasions, result in extreme instances of happiness and joy too. It depends upon what sort of 'life space' or cognitive organization one already has. If the cognitive organisation that one already has is in the direction of negative expectation perceptual incongruences in such a case may give rise to moments of extreme happiness.

Secondary anxiety, on the other hand, is defined by McReynolds as "adventitious pairing of neutral stimuli with extremely high instances of primary anxiety. Secondary anxiety, therefore, is conditioned anxiety in Pavlovian sense.

Averill (Zukerman and Spielberger, 1976), differing slightly with McReynolds, defines anxiety as "entailing a disintegration of cognitive systems related to personal identity." He does not talk of anxiety purely as a negative affect. The possibility of anxiety exists whenever an individual is unable to assign "meaning" to his world because of unstable or conflicting cognitive structures. He further holds that "highly creative thought may be fluid and unstable, at least in its formative stages. Perhaps, this is the reason why anxiety is often a central theme in the writings of highly creative individuals viz., Kierkegaard, Camus, Sartre and Dostoevski—to name a few" (p. 121).

Regarding the source of anxiety, Averill says that any condition which significantly impairs the ability of the individual to process information and to meaningfully interpret his environment, in the context of personal identity may be potential source of anxiety. In any case of anxiety the ultimate impairment must be viewed in terms of dialectic between the individual and his environment. The potential for anxiety exists whenever, and for whatever reason, this dialectic is broken.

Fischer (1970) examines the concepts of anxiety from various viewpoints and offers, what he calls, "Integrative" view of anxiety. He defines anxiety as "the experience of being impelled to actualize for which my abilities have already been apprehended as uncertain."

In Fischer's definition the term "uncertain" is very important. Verily, it is the apprehension of uncertainty that is responsible for ensuing of anxiety. If one were certain of success there would not have been any question of being anxious. And even if one were sure of failure, the need to become anxious would not arise. But the point on which Fischer can be criticized is his view of circumscribing the area of anxiety to one's abilities alone ; for, the successful accomplishment of what one wants to actualize does not depend merely on one's abilities. The success in an endeavour is a function of a host of other factors, including the chance factors. Second, Fischer's definition seems to fall short of more comprehensive connotation. There is no indication, whatsoever, how the "failure to actualize" what one wants to actualize is going to affect "me". Therefore, to hold that anxiety experiencing is because of the apprehended uncertainty of "my abilities" may not cover sufficient ground. It involves more complex configuration of which, no doubt, "my abilities" and competence are significant aspects.

There seems another limitation of such a definition. The scope of anxiety in such a situation cannot be extended beyond "test anxiety". Other types of anxiety find no explanation under such a definition. Does anxiety ensure only when the question of abilities is involved ? Freud's "moral anxiety" and Schachtel's "separation anxiety" have no place in Fischer's concept of anxiety, whereas the fact is that these two areas warrant sufficient evidence of the experience of anxiety.

The various viewpoints tending to illuminate the nature and cause of anxiety may appear divergent. They, infact, reveal the different facets of the same phenomenon and hence are free from any conflict or contradiction. Syadvada – the great oriental "Jain" philosophy lends an explanation of such seeming divergence, according to which one can perceive reality only partially. What is needed in this context is the desirability of a more comprehensive view which can take into account a larger number of aspects associated with the phenomenon. What is attempted below is a synthesis of different viewpoints in order to arrive at a fuller conceptualization of the experience of anxiety.

Despite the variations in outlook, the different thinkers have on the notion of anxiety and its cause(s), they show little divergence, in distinguishing the experience of anxiety and the experience of fear. Also, there is little controversy over what may be called the "manifest symptomology of anxiety," that is, its psychosomatic determinants. Given two situations—one involving fear and the other, anxiety—one can unmistakenly distinguish between them. One can clearly indicate the danger involved in a fear situation, but what is at stake in an anxiety experience is highly debatable and controversial.

In the fear situation the threat is to the physical organism and hence, such a threat can be clearly and specifically located. The threat is to what exists spatio-temporally. The fear situation as well as what is threatened, are objective realities. In such a case, there is often a tendency to "flee away" from the situation in order to preserve oneself. The fear situation is not there because of any choice or participation of the individual. It just occurs or happens.

In an anxiety situation, on the other hand, the threat does not exist "out there" ; it is only imagined and subjectively apprehended. The situation involving anxiety occurs because of individual's own choice, and hence, it is his own creation. The tendency in such a situation, therefore, is to confront it and not to flee away from it.

Besides, apprehension of threat in the anxiety situation is not to the "physical organism" but to the psychological self of the individual. The psychological self, as we know, comprises the totality of relationships with the physical and social environment of the individual. It may be expressed as the, "I", "me" "mine" etc. Truely, the individual self is sustained by the constellations of relationship with the world of "they". In the event of threat to these constellations the individual feels a sense of meaninglessness. It is for this reason that what is threatened in anxiety situation cannot be specifically located.

On the basis of this analysis we can hold that while fear is a perceived threat to the biological self, anxiety is a subjectively apprehended threat to the psychological self. This apprehension surfaces due to the uncertainty of not being able to preserve what one psychologically 'is,' or, not being able to actualize what one potentially 'is.'

Having thus attempted to differentiate fear from anxiety let us now try to trace more specific referents of anxiety in order to arrive at comprehensive definition of it. We can do so this analysis by explicitly stating the basic assumptions underlying human predicament in which man, of necessity, finds himself as an ontological "being".

The first assumption is that man as a phenomenological self exists in a social matrix with complexity of involvements with other "beings", and things. Second, he inherently needs appreciation and approbation of all his actions from those he considers significant ; conversely, he does not will to be deprecated or disapproved for his actions. Third, embeddedness is a precondition to man's existence, and it is symbiotically related to his ontological freedom. With these assumptions, we can now proceed to understand the nature and cause(s) of anxiety.

Analysis of anxiety from one angle reveals that social context is the essential background in which it happens to ensue. Without consideration of a social living anxiety cannot and does not occur. Second, uncertainty of results/consequences of one's self initiated actions (if such action are involved) is the necessary condition, of its occurrence. In most cases, an individual feels anxious because of apprehension of his being disapproved by "significant others". The first source of anxiety lies in the conflict between (in Freudian terminology) the Id and the Super-ego. It is a fear of disapproval by significant others associated with the way (means) of instinctual gratification. Freud called this anxiety *Moral Anxiety* which ultimately leads to meaninglessness of the self via its repercussion on one's moral worth.

The other source of anxiety is due to the subjective feeling of uncertainty when one attempts to actualize what one wills to actualize. It is also an apprehension of being disapproved in the event of failure. The individual, in such a situation, is haunted by the apprehension about what would happen should his abilities fail him. It is observed that inferior self-perception is the basis of this kind of anxiety, and the main area is of human competence. Fischer (1970) is the originator of this idea. I call such an anxiety as "Inferiority Anxiety" ; for the very idea of failure of what one wills to actualize makes one feel inferior to others and hence, anxious. This kind of anxiety also, ultimately, leads towards meaninglessness of the self but via its reprecussions on one's competence viz. physical/intellectual worth.

The above two sources of anxiety, obviously, emerge from the first two assumptions. There is a third source of anxiety too which is inherent in and springs from the third assumption. This kind of anxiety is due to apprehension of being unembedded from what the individual thinks sustain him. It is not associated with social disapproval neither involves 'willed' actions. I call this anxiety as "*Separation Anxiety*". The idea of being separated from the state of embeddedness makes one anxious via repercussions on one's security.

Interestingly, the three kinds of anxiety, viz. the Moral Anxiety, the Inferiority Anxiety, and the Separation Anxiety, can be traced to be aetiologically associated with gratification of human needs. It is a truism that human actions are impelled/ prompted by need satisfaction/reduction ; and as is clear from above, the actions responsible for ensuing of anxiety are self-willed. Such actions may be due to some physiological or psychological compulsion of the individual. Actions prompted by physiological compulsion aim at preservation and strengthening of the biological self, and in their effects, they are most natural and spontaneous : they tend to satisfy needs like hunger, oxygen, sex etc. Actions prompted by psychological compulsion, on the other hand, aim at preservation and strengthening of psychological self. The status seeking behaviour of man, his urge to be superior to others (behaviour of competitive type) etc. fall in this category of psychological needs. Such needs are specifically the needs of the homo-sapiens, and are distinct from those of other animals. These are acquired during the course of one's development as a social being; and are triggered off by 'human motivation to achieve' and his general sensitivity.

Satisfaction or reduction of a need is the goal of human activity, but for achievement of a goal one needs some "means." In the case of goal achievement there are two possibilities : one can either be confident of goal achievement or be uncertain about it. Occurrence of anxiety is possible in the latter case because, non-achievement of goals has direct repercussions on one's adequacy as self ; it is a function of, at least, two important factors viz., motivation and his self-perception. The anxiety caused due to apprehension about the achievement of the goal as such constitutes Inferiority Anxiety.

The Moral Anxiety on the other hand, ensues when chosen means to an end in the way of need satisfaction (reduction) are not socially desirable ; it does not matter whether the need is truely biological, psychological or otherwise. It is always the unworthiness of the means to the end that is responsible for moral anxiety. It must be clearly understood that the end (need satisfaction or reduction) per se is an ontological necessity and, hence, it is amoral in nature ; that is, the end by itself is beyond any moral scrutiny.

Apart from biological and psychological needs, there may be third category of needs in this hierarchy manifested through one's associations with other "beings", "things", "beliefs" or "faiths". These may be named *socio-cultural* needs of an individual. These are the areas where an individual finds himself embedded to and which he thinks sustain him. These needs, in their effects, are security providing. This embeddedness, according to Schachtel, "starts with intra-uterine existence" and continues throughout life. Any situation wherein one apprehends a fear of being unembedded is anxiety producing. While in the case of 'Moral' and 'Inferioriy' Anxiety the criterion of anxiety is deprecation or disapproval of the individual by significant others, occasioned by self-willed actions ; Separation Anxiety, on the other hand, is due to the fear of being separated from the "intactness", the "embeddedness" as a result of changes in the physical and social environment brought about by forces external to the individual.

In this hierarchy of needs one can go still higher. There are needs directed towards satisfaction of transcendental or spiritual self : the same may be called super-individual or transcendental needs. But being beyond any social context they have nothing to do with anxiety.

The above discussion leading to various types of anxiety (each type having a difference source), enables us to formulate a general definition of anxiety. One can hold that *anxiety is a felt apprehension of some threat to moral integrity, competence, or embeddedness of a person.* The integrity, competence, and embeddedness determine the general "security base" of a person. Obviously such a definition of anxiety is not a new or a unique one ; nevertheless, what was implicit and global in Rollo May's concept of 'security base' becomes explicit here, for, the ground that constitutes one's security is not physical but rather psychological. Even statements like "X" is a good person, or "X" is a competent person are in a way security providing.

The security base (the psychological self) comprising the above three components sustains the individual by providing a meaning to it at psychological level. It is for this reason that the threat of anxiety tends to bring meaninglessness and insignificance. Most philosopher-psychologists hold this view. To the author this takes care of all other possible aspects of the self which may be said to be in danger in a situation that is anxiety-producing. In fact, other aspects of the self, if any, can be subsumed under any of these three components.

Now question may arise whether the explanation of the cause of anxiety in terms of disturbance in the security base is absolute and final ? The next querry in this direction may be, "why do we need security at all ? And the only answer may be that we need security because we want to live and live with freedom. That is, the security base protects one's ontological freedom which is uniquely human. It is for this reason that anxiety is sui-generis and an cntirely human phenomenon. In the final analysis, therefore, it is the ontological freedom of man which gives meaning and significance to his self. Apprehension of threat to the psychological security base ultimately springs from threat to the ontological freedom which is essentially covert, implicit and unconscious with the human organism. It is for this reason that the experience of anxiety is never specific but global and nebulous.

It may be mentioned that at the psychological plane it may be the ontological freedom with which man is immediately and consciously concerned. It is only the logical extension of what is "given". What is psychologically "given" is the feeling of apprehension caused due to uncertainty of results concerning one's competence, moral integrity, and embeddedness.

It is worthy to note that in an anxiety situation, unless the threat is exceedingly powerful (which may lead to dissolution of the self), there is natural tendency to thwart such a threat. This is because one wants to save one's "self" from being reduced to meaninglessness and insignificance. Instead of fleeing away from anxiety producing situation one tends to confront it. Existentialist thinkers such as Kierkegaard, Heidegar etc. and the psychological philosophers such as Schachtel, Fromm and Horney rightly associate anxiety with the essential conditions of human growth and development mediated by freedom choice responsibility individuation etc.

Causes of Anxiety

Whenever a phenomenon occurs there are various aspects related to it which can be said to be responsible for its occurrence. Any thing that is responsible for change, motion or action may, in general, be termed as the cause, and the "change" or "effect" may be associated with energy or action, whether or not connected with matter. Leubipus was first to give a clear formulation that nothing happens without a ground. Aristotle distinguished four types of causes. J.S. Mill also subscribed to the theory of plurality of causes contending that an effect may be produced by variety of causes.

The question of the "cause" of anxiety has remained quite controversial. Probably a better light can be shed on the phenomenon of anxiety, if it is analysed in line with theory of plurality of causes. One may venture to analyse the cause of anxiety following Aristotelian lines of the "types" of causes in terms of *efficient cause, material cause, "formal cause"* and the *final cause.**

In the opening paragraph of this section anxiety was called

* 1. Efficient cause is that by which any change is brought about : it is the force or the agent that produces the effect.
2. Material cause is that out of which some thing arises.
3. Formal cause is the act or the pattern or essence which determines the creation of the effect.
4. Final cause is the purpose because of which the change (effect occurs).

"sui-generis," a unique phenomenon. One explanation for this may be that it occurs prior to the act or the event responsible for its causation. The cause of anxiety lies in the effects : One feels anxious for the fear of effects. Normally we know that the antecedent is the cause and consequent is the effect. I get hurt and I feel pain. Here pain is the effect which occurs after my getting hurt (the antecedent). So the cause of pain occurs before it (pain) temporally. Whereas in the case of anxiety, it, occurs prior to because of which it occurs.

The three types of anxiety discussed above can be causally analysed by examining the background under which each type occurs.

In the case of "moral anxiety" one tends to do something for the sake of need gratification prompted (obviously) by "Id". In an attempt to do so one gets anxious by the apprehension of being ridiculed, deprecated, or condemned by the "significant others" for one's choice of the socially undesirable way of need gratification. Here, what drives the individual to do the act is the desire of need gratification which per se is morally neutral, yet, being the force behind the act is the *efficient* cause of moral anxiety. The 'way' adopted for such need gratification becomes the "*formal cause*," because, had one chosen a socially approved 'way,' anxiety would not have occurred. Fear of being ridiculed, condemned etc. by the significant others is the *material* cause of anxiety (in the sense of what matters to the individual at mundane level). And finally, the ontological freedom getting restricted through the material consequences of the act becomes the *final cause* of anxiety.

In the case of "inferiority" anxiety one tends to do something which is necessary for his growth and, hence, socially appreciable. But the measures of such growth are the 'others' who constitute his psychological environment. One wants to grow higher in relation to others. The successful completion of this act will elevate him in his own eyes as well as in the eyes of those significantly related to him. This growth may speak of his competence or ability. But failure to effectively do the act may undermine his competence in the eyes of others as perceived by him. So, it is a situation that involves test of one's competence.

In this kind of anxiety, therefore, the tendency, desire or the motivation to grow higher in relation to others is the *efficient* cause, because, it makes him compete with others. The apprehension of failure of one's abilities constitutes the *formal* cause of anxiety. The consequence of such apprehension of failure, viz., fear of being ridiculed, condemned etc. by significant others is the *material* cause of anxiety. And the consequence of material cause of anxiety viz., restriction of ontological freedom, is the *final* cause of inferiority anxiety.

The third source of anxiety lies in the apprehension of being unembedded from some "beings", objects or relationship etc. to which one is psychologically attached. The fear of being separated from such objects etc., is a distressing experience designated here as separation anxiety. The objects etc. to which one gets attached during the course of life may be material objects like wealth, property or "beings" or relationships such/ as status position. All these factors to which one tends to cling to provide him specific security patterns. Any situation involving a threat of being separated from these mundane attachments will be anxiety/producing, in proportion with the magnitude of attachments.

Here, the abrupt change in the environment and the factors responsible for such a change constitute the "efficient" cause of separation anxiety. The apprehension of loss of property and/ or relationships etc. with which one is embedded is the "material" cause of anxiety. The "formal" cause of anxiety is the resultant feeling of insecurity and lonliness. And the "final" cause lies in the ultimate consequences of this disequilibrium i.e. curtailment of one's ontological freedom.

The separation anxiety may be causally distinguishable from the other two kinds, in that, the efficient cause may also lie external to the individual, while the forces causing moral or inferiority anxiety lie within the individual itself. The force responsible for apprehended separation from embeddedness may be some condition of the physical or social environment beyond any control of the individual.

As is obvious from the above discussion on the subject of anxiety, the nomenclature given to the three types of anxiety is based on what is directly apprehended i.e., the formal cause : moral anxiety ensues because of apprehension of losing moral integrity ; in inferiority anxiety it is apprehension of becoming inferior to others, whereas, in the separation anxiety it is the apprehension of being separated from those aspects of the mundane world to which one wants to remain embedded.

Having thus delineated the basic assumptions concerning human nature, the types of anxiety-experience, and the conditions under which each type of anxiety occurs, we can hopefully attempt to define anxiety experience more comprehensively in the following manner :

Anxiety-experience is a distressing psycho-physiological reaction of an individual ensuing because of the apprehended uncertainty of one's (i) moral integrity, (ii) competence, and (iii) embeddedness.

Human Personality Dimensions—An Overview

The whole discussion on the two concepts viz., anxiety and creativity, seems to converge to the following points :

1. In the phenomenon of creativity the use of "*primary process thinking*" seems essential, though, not sufficient : some unconscious, or, at least, subconscious mental mechanisms are at work when a creative idea emerges. The second implication is that the life of a creative person is not free from some sort of conflicts, cognitive or of some other kind like tension, problem of adjustment etc.

2. Anxiety (as a state or a trait), in itself, cannot be designated as derogatory or contributory (facilitating) to human growth and development. Depending upon the situation, life history and inherited dispositions, etc. of the individual, it can act both ways. That is, if the individual is overwhelmed by anxiety he may turn neurotic or psychotic. The same

anxiety, on the other hand, may lead to creativeness of a high order if one constantly confronts it. It all depends, probably, upon the type of person one is.

The concept of "type" has fared very badly at the hands of psychologists. According to Stagnen (1948) the shift from *type* to *trait* conceptions has generally paralleled the progress of psychology. Eysenck (1970) examines in detail the modern typologies of personality, particularly as given by Jung (1921) and Kretschmer (1948), and finally gives, what he thinks, a correct position regarding the concept of "type" in personality organisation. Drawing much from different thinkers and using factor analytic studies, Eysenck (1970) defines a "type" as a "group of correlated traits", in the same manner as a trait is defined as "a group of correlated behavioural acts."

Eysenck's latest organisation of emotive human personality consists of three types which can be expressed in the form of three dimensions, orthogonal to each other. These are *Extraversion*, *Neuroticism*, and *Psychoticism*. Every human being has all these dimensions in varying degrees. Each dimension has two extremes which are only hypothetical constructs. These 'extremes' are Extraversion Introversion, stability-instability, Tough mindedness – tender mindedness.

In conceptualizing these three dimensions of personality Eysenck has drawn much from other theorists viz. Jordon (1890), Gross (1902), Jung (1921), Allport (1937), and Kretshmer (1948). Extraversion –Introversion concepts of Jung, active unimpassioned concept of Jordon, broad-shallow and narrow-deep concept of Gross respectively share many things in common. These concepts, however, are not psychometrically pure, since they are not orthogonal to each other. Eysenck's "types" differ significantly from what the above theorists asserted. What Eysenck calls hysterics (extraverted neurotics) are a prototype for the "Extravert" of Jung. In the same fashion, Introvert of Jung is a "dysthemic" (Introverted neurotic) of Eysenck. In making these types more explcit, he draws upon Hull and Pavlov ; and thus relates the developments of these types to physiology and learning theory as primarily expounded by Hull. Using the concept of *reactive inhibition* Eysenck gives a general law that explains development of extroversion-introversion dimension based on the law of *excitation-inhibition.* He states :

"Individuals in whom reactive inhibition is generated quickly, in whom strong reactive inhibitions are generated and in whom reactive inhibition is dissipated slowly are, thereby, predisposed to extraverted pattern of behaviour, and to develop hysterical disorders in the case of naurotic break down ; conversely, individuals in whom reactive inhibition is generated slowly, in whom reactive inhibition is dissipated quickly are, thereby, predisposed to develop introverted patterns of behaviour, and to develop dysthemic disorders in the case of neurotic break down" (Eysenck 1971 p. 214). Eysenck differs with other such theorists in regard to abnormality. Jung and Kretschmer believe that the neurotic and psychotic disorders lie along the same continuum of abnormality, whereas, in Eysenck's system these two are qualitatively different from one another. To quote Eysenck, (op. cit. p. 214) "neurosis is not an intermediary resting place on the road that leads from normal behaviour to abnormal but its roots are already inherited in the form of neuroticism—the emotional lability." Similarly psychoticism is an independent personality factor characterized by rigidity, cruelty tough-mindedness, insensitivity, apathy and the like. These two disorders result because of quantitative divergence from normal idiosyncracies—the inherited dispositions—which in lesser or greater degrees, are present in all human beings at birth.

CHAPTER III

Survey of Related Studies

A perusal of related research studies in the field reveals that significantly such studies cover three areas. These areas include (i) predictive characteristics, (ii) criteria of creativity, and (iii) the environmental factors that can modify the relation between predictors and the criteria, such as education and training, working conditions, etc. Furthermore, the findings of the studies which relate personality traits to creative thinking abilities are not conclusive ; and in many cases, seem to suggest contradictory viewpoints. The widest variance appears when one compares the personality traits of 'known groups of adults' engaged in performances of tasks of creative nature and individuals showing creative thinking abilities on certain tests that are designed to measure such abilities. For example, some studies show that creative adults (judged on the basis of their actual creative products) are highly introvert and show normal to high anxiety or neuroticism ; while adults showing creative potential, as measured on certain tests and inventories, show extraverted behaviour to a larger extent, and are less anxious than persons whom Maslow calls "self-actualized" creatives.

Research Articles and Reviews, Showing the Existence of Sub-conscious, Unconscious Mental Mechanisms in Creativity

Brand Harry (1976) tries to demonstrate how creative expression and its manifestation occur concomitantly with certain persons having neurotic tendencies. He describes Franz Kafka as the most representative prose writer of the

20th century. His personal conflicts, especially with his parents, are revealed in his writings. Even in the midst of severe neurotic symptoms, such as his irrational anxiety, paranoia, and hysteria, Kafka was able to write in a clear and firm style which had universal acceptance and meaning. According to Harry, such a finding proves the existence and role of unconscious and subconscious processes in creative thought expression. It is these processes that give a unique direction to one's manifestations of innate capacity. One may, therefore, hypothesize that in certain cases the existence of anxiety and conflict becomes an occasion to kindle what is hidden in the innermost recesses of the psyche.

But in Jane's (1977) study the above conclusion seems to be contradicted. According to Jane, who discusses the relationship between creativity and "altered states of consciousness," occurring in dreams and meditation, hypnosis, and biofeedback, severely conflicted individuals cannot cope with the altered states of consciousness. Such individuals are less creative than healthy persons.

Muller-Braunschweig (1975), in a research article discusses the occurrence of creative powers and psychopathology in the same personality. According to him, the creative Ego must be flexible, dealing with Id created unconscious fantasies in a comparatively free way, but in psychopathology this ability is impaired. Nevertheless, creative functions may be formed which act to work out anxiety-ladden fantasies in a world of symbols, thus, enabling the Ego to deal freely with impluses. As a work of art develops objectification of fantasies brings forth a new reality. Intensification of cathexis and simultaneous displacement of substitute objects is posited as a condition for later creative processes, particularly, artistic ones.

Perry (1973) in an article "Creative Element in Madness" states that the deepest experiences of the psychic life cannot be communicated in every day words but require a new language. The psychotic, immersed in his inner spaces, is lonely, because he cannot tell his experiences to those who are not living at the same level. Drawing a similarity between creativity and schizophrenia, the author holds that both these psychic processes deal with integration, dis-integration and reintegration. In both of these processes "affect images" emerge rather than certain themes. These are followed by clashing and resolution ; and finally a rebirth emerges.

Domino (1977) examined the existence of "primary process" thinking in dreams, and their relationship to creative achievement. He compared the night dreams as reported by 38 high school males who were considered creative (according to teachers reports and RAT scores). Dreams report of these creative subjects were rated by clinical psychologists as exhibiting greater "primary process" thinking than those of matched controls. Their dream protocols also included a significant greater proportion of symbolism, condensation, and unusual combinations, but a smaller proportion of contradictions. In this experiment the presence of "primary process" thinking was found to be significantly related to creativity level.

Hammer (1975), in a research article entitled, "Artistic Creativity—Giftedness or Sickness," discusses the relationship between creativity, mental health or illness and emotional conflict. It is concluded that (a) for each individual there is an optimal level of tension and anxiety that is necessary for personal growth and creativity, (b) the ability to synthesize and to integrate is necessary for creative work, (c) the capacity to be in touch with deep unconscious forces, without breaking down, is crucial to an artist.

Creativity and Activation—Empirical Studies

Vos (1977) experimentally tested the effect of activation on creativity (creative potential) to verify the hypothesis that an inverted U-shaped function exists between creativity and activation (Yerkes - Dodson Law), according to which a low level of drive facilitates creative thinking only slightly, because, the motivation it provides is inadequate to effect performance. A high drive level interferes with creative process functioning such that performance is similar to or worse than that obtained with low drive level. Therefore, the level of drive which stimulates optimal performance lies somewhere in the middle range of the drive.

Vos took 30 male undergraudates at the University of Mainz (Germany) on a random basis. The subjects were assigned to three conditions of low (relaxed, friendly atmosphere), middle (test-like situation), and high level of activation. Instruments used to measure creativity were AC test of Creative Thinking, and German version of RAT (Remote Association Test). Dependent variables were : ideational fluency, originality, spontaneous flexibility, and RAT Scores.

Results from Vos's study confirm the hypothesis for ideational fluency, and are interpreted on the basis of two distinct processes which may determine creative thinking of the fluency type in activational states, and can be associated with different kinds of attention deployment.

Martindale (1975, pp. 71-79) reviews theoretical and empirical reasons for expecting a relationship between creativity and level of arousal. The results of six published studies, exploring the relationship between creativity and psychophysiological variables (EEG and GSR), are also reviewed. According to interpretations done by Martindale, creative subjects tend to have high "resting or based" level arousal to be physiologically over-reactive to stimulation ; and perform relatively poorly on biofeed-back tasks. The largest and the most consistent EEG differences between creative and non-creative subjects occur during task performance. Non-creative subjects tend to show Alpha blocking on cognitive tasks while creative subjects tend to be differently reactive. During tasks that do not call for or allow creativity, they too exhibit Alpha blocking. However, they tend to operate at a relatively low level of arousal, and show Alpha enhancement during tasks that call for or allow creativity.

Drwal (1975) examined three groups with a view to study influences of emotional processes on creative thinking. The emotional factors considered were activation, motivation and emotional stress. It was inferred that (a) Creativity is facilitated by non-emotional activation, positive emotions, intrinsic motivations, task involvement, resistance to stress, non-conforming attitude, independence, and achievement orientation ; (b) Evaluation of ideas is affected by emotions. Social pressures anxiety and fear make the ideas conservative and vigorous.

Personality Studies of 'Known Groups of Creatives'

Kretschmer (1933) reported that the commonly held notion of associating mental sickness with creativity is not valid. He found out that scientists are not associated with any kind of such abnormality. To quote Kretschmer, scientists have shown "lively originality and vibrate with sensibility and inward tension . . . . Behind the cool stream of thought there lies a glowing passionate core . . . . that drives their thoughts . . . . Scientific and inventive genius is . . . . under the sway of an over-valued idea. The success of such an idea depends upon the favourableness of circumstances and the intellectual power of the individual. The successful are inventors . . . . the failures paranoids." In fact, Kretschmer seems to indirectly favour proneness towards abnormality of behaviour as a characteristic of the creative genius, which may become manifest under the away of circumstances that lead to failure.

Roe (1952) did an extensive study of the men of science and tried to give a common pattern of a typical eminent scientist, inspite of the individual and professional differences existing among them. The characteristic nature of a typical eminent scientist can be inferred from the following description given by Roe.

"He is the first born child of a middle class family, the son of a professional man. He is likely to have been a sickly child or to have lost a parent at an early age. He has a very high I.Q. ; and in boyhood began to do a great deal of reading. He tended to feel lonely and indifferent, and to be shy and aloof from his classmates. He had only a moderate interest in girls . . . . Not until his junior or senior year in college did he decide on his vocation as a scientist. What decided him (almost invariably) was a college project in whlch he had occasion to do some independent research work . . . . to find out things for himself. Once he discovered the pleasure of this kind of work, he never turned back. He is completely satisfied with his chosen vocation (only one of 64 eminent scientists - a Nobel Prize winner—says he would have preferred to do something else. He wanted to be a farmer but could not make a living at it). He works hard and devotedly in his laboratory, often seven days a week. He says his work is his life and he has few recreations, these being restricted to fishing, sailing, walking or some other individualistic activities. Better than any other interest or activity, scientific research seems to meet the inner need of his nature" (Roe 1952, p. 187).

Stein (1956) studied industrial research chemists, as rated on creativity, both by superior colleagues and subordinates. His investigations clearly show that more creative chemists tend to be more autonomous, striving for more distant goals ; have more integrative attitudes ; are more cautious and realistic ; have more differentiated value heirarchy ; and perceive themselves as assertive and authoritative with leadership ability.

Similarly Gough (1961), on the basis of his investigations, reported that eminent scientists have characteristics similar to those of creative workers in other fields. These characteristics were : high intelligence, strong tendency towards independent judgements and achievement, personal dominance, responsiveness to other people and motives, and a marked preference for aesthetics and complexity of design. Gough's explorations show that the impluse to creativity in science is derived from the same force in the dynamics of a person as creativity in other fields, and contradicts the commonplace view that creativity in science is different from creativity in other fields, in so far as dynamics of human behaviour is concerned.

Cattell's contributions (Cattell and Drevdahl, 1955) give slightly different dimensions in comparison to what Stein and Gough have reported. He found the creative scientist highly intelligent, possessing independence of mind and dominance, as well as emotional sensitivity. But in comparison to general population, the scientists were found to be introspective, reserved and cool They tend to be outwardly inhibited, serious and taciturn, and self-sufficient to a degree. They have disregard for social pleasantries as well as conventions. Cattell illustrated this fact by citing Cavendish's examples : when he was asked to attend a formal social gathering, arranged for foreign scientists at Cambridge, he broke away and ran down by corridor "squeaking like a bat" (p. 248-61).

Taylor and Barron (1963), referring to summary papers which originally were presented at the Utah Conference on Scientific Creativity, reveal some comprehensive results. According to these reports, scientists are characterized by a high degree of autonomy, preference for mental manipulations involving things rather than people, high Ego-strength, emotional stability, liking for method and precision, preference for defence mechanisms, such as *repression* and *isolation*, a high degree of impulse control, a liking for abstract thinking with considerable tolerance for cognitive ambiguity, independence of judgement, a drive towards comprehensiveness, and an interest in coping with uncertain circumstances.

Cattell (1968), on the basis of biographies of scientists, concluded that scientific researchers are found to be schizothemes, withdrawn, skeptical, internally pre-occupied, precise and reliable. The average level of Ego-strength and emotional stability are distinctly higher for effective scientific researchers than for the general population. They are found to have high anxiety level, high irritability and excitability. In an earlier study, Cattell (1959), on the basis of investigations, made on 144 physicists, biologists and psychologists, seems to arrive at the following conclusions : (a) personality profiles of these researchers differ significantly at .01 level from that of an average man, in as much as, they are more schizotheme, intelligent, dominant, inhibited, emotionally sensitive, and radical ; (b) the researchers' personality profiles differ from those of equal general intelligence who are outstanding in administration and teaching, in the sense that former are schizotheme, emotionally less stable, more radical, and uniformly lower on all primary personality factors of extraversion. In an attempt to compare personality pattern of research scientists in American universities with those of university teachers and administrators, and also with average scores of general population, Cattell and Drevdahl (1955) observed the research scientists to be significantly high on factors of schizotheme (Factor A), and self-sufficiency (Factor Q_2) as contrasted with college groups of administrators. The differences on schizotheme and self-sufficiency have also been observed by Drevdahl in a comparison of creative and non-creative students in Science and Art subjects.

MacKinnon (1962), in his sample of master architects, finds them to enjoy sensuous experience, to have social poise and presence, to be genuinly dependable and responsible. They tend to be critical, skeptical and not easily impressed by and concerned with their own adequacy as a person. On the basis of psychological tests it is shown that the creative groups have greater psychopathology than the representative members of the same profession. The average creative architect is less marked by deviant behaviour, but is still consistently and substantially higher on psychopathological dispositions, and strikingly higher on "ego-strength" than general population.

In another study, MacKinnon (1962) selected two additional samples (group II and group III), both of which matched the highly creative sample of nominated architects (Group I), with respect to age and geographic location of practice. Group II and III respectively represented less eminent architects and ordinary architects.

The male creative group, demonstrates extremely high peak on the Mf (femininity) scale of the "California Psychological Inventory" (1957) and of the "Masculinity—Femininity" scale of "Strong's Vocational Interest Blank" (Strong, 1959). The study reveals that the more creative a person is, the more he reveals an openness to his own feelings and emotions, has a sensitive intellect and understanding, self-awareness and wide ranging interests, including many which, in the American culture, are considered feminine (MacKinnon, 1962).

Other similar investigations were made by MacKinnon (1962) and Barron (1965) on mathematicians and writers. On the basis of these investigations creative mathematicians were found to be significantly different from other representatives of their professions in being more individualistic, pre-occupied, artistic, complicated, courageous, emotional, imaginative and self-centred. The creative mathematicians were also high both on theoretical and aesthetic values, as well as, on psychological measures of MMPI. Furthermore, they had high degree of Ego-strength. The results for creative writers were similar to those obtained on architects and mathematicians. The creative writers were found to have a high degree of intellectual ability, verbal fluency, and tendency for aesthetic reaction. They valued intellectual and cognitive matters, and autonomy. The group, in itself, was interesting and straightforward in dealing with others, and consistent with standards of behaviour. The average creative writer was high on all measures of psychopathology as compared to general population. In this case, again, the creative writers were found to have high ego-strength.

Roy Chaudhary (1961, 65) conducted a number of studies on artistic creativity and personality correlates, individually and in collaboration with some others, namely, Ganguly and Bhattacharya. He is thought to be pioneer of creativity studies in India. His explorations have largely been in the area of personality of artists, especially musicians. The major personality characteristics of the creative artists, according to Roy Chaudhary, are : sensitivity, wide spectrum of interests, emotional involvement with work, femininity, non-conformity, love for originality, withdrawn tendency, and high Ego-strength.

Jha (1978) studied the personality characteristics of 38 creative persons living in Western India. They were national award winners in various fields, including artists, literary figures, film directors, military generals, and others. The Q-sort methodology was selected for the study, and Jung's typology was used in relation to creativity. This included independence, attitudes, mechanisms and functions, levels of introversion-extroversion, consciousness-unconsciousness, thinking, feeling, sensations and intuitions. Findings of his study are consistent with some of the conclusions arrived at by

Maslow (1962) whose findings have been quoted elsewhere in Chapter I of this study.

In a study of Drevdahl (1964) the creative group of psychologists appears to be more interested in scientific investigations than in a more socially oriented activity. These psychlogists are characterized by relative unconcern of other people, authority, rules, regulations, restrictions, and the like, indicating a definite degree of independence. Their personal, social and emotional adjustment is found to be superior to that of less eminent counterparts. They are usually self-oriented without showing concern to such things as social and sexual relationship, public and professional criticism. Moral and social responsibility is generally accepted by them without excessive concern. Other studies by Drevdahl and Cattell (1958) on artists and writers, and by Cross et al. (1967) on creative artists, the results obtained confirm the findings by Cattell (1959). In general all these studies reveal the creative person to be introverted and anxious and having a high degree of ego-strength. Cross et al. (1967) further remark that the artists differ on all the personality factors except intelligence. One of the largest differences that has been noticed on artistic tendency and historical unconcern is factor M.

Tripathi (1973, 1976, 1979) conducted biographical studies on creative writers in India, for the purpose of evaluating personality factors conducive to creative writing. He used both the interview techniques and the personality tests. The main findings of his research are as follows :

1. The Introversion-extroversion dimension of personality is relevant to creative production in writing. Introversion provides the necessary conditions for dwelling in the world of ideas, and is decidely more favourable. Extraversion also impels one to write ; and there are areas and themes where a writer with extraverted personality may be at an advantage.

2. The basic motivation for creative writing exists in the psyche of the writer in the form of guilt feelings, which find their partial appeasement through his extraverted writing. Tension appears to be a kind of condition which may find its

release in writing, probably, more in poetry than in prose. At times creative writing is the only solace of a troubled mind.

Personality Studies of Potentially Creative Individuals

The research studies noted above deal with the findings of investigations done on "known groups" of creative persons, i.e. of those whose potential was manifest. What is of greater concern to the investigator is to know what personality correlates are associated with potentially high creative persons.

As is evident from the studies mentioned earlier, there is not much consistency among personality correlates of "known groups" of creatives in themselves. The difference seems to magnify when the personality correlates of the potentially creative persons are compared with those of 'known groups' of creatives. White (1968) brings this distinction to limelight when he says that personality correlates of creative behaviour, as determined by known groups of creative individuals are, in most cases, distinctly opposed to personality correlates of creative behaviour as identified by divergent thinking tests. For example, extraverts, as defined through Cattell's 16 Personality Factors, are higher on divergent thinking measures of fluency, flexibility and originality than introverts.

Kinnard White (1976) conducted another study to find out the relationship between anxiety, extraversion-introversion and divergent thinking. He tested hypotheses concerning the effects of anxiety level and its interaction with extraversion-introversion. The rationale for testing hypotheses, concerning anxiety and divergent thinking, derives from Spence (1956) who suggests that anxiety is a drive, and very strong drives or high levels of anxiety can prevent adaptive changes in behaviour.

White took two hundred male fresh-men as subjects at the University of North Carolina. The independent variables were all derived from 16 PF questionnaire, Form A (Cattell and Eber 1967). Subjects were assessed on two divergent thinking tasks which yielded three types of scores, namely, *spontaneous verbal flexibility, ideational fluency, and originality,*

The results show that regarding significant main effects the low anxiety group scored higher on the ideational fluency tasks than the higher anxiety group. And the high E-1 (Extraversion-Introversion) group scored higher on ideational fluency tasks. Furthermore, the differentially high performance on originality tasks was made by the low anxiety group (The High E-1 sub-group was the primary contributor to significant interaction effects). In this way White substantiates (though, only partially) the findings of Spence (1964), Cattell and Scheier (1961), Eysenck and Eysenck (1962).

Kendil and Torrance (1978) conducted a study to verify as to what extent Finch's (1977) findings were true. Finch (1977) had reported that socially and emotionally mal-adjusted children have higher creative potential than socially and emotionally adjusted children. The investigators selected 50 children as subjects. These were drawn from grade one through grade five of special public school meant for emotionally disturbed and behaviour disordered children. Each child was tested individually on TTCT (Torrance Tests of Creative Thinking). Scores on fluency, flexibility and originality were compared with national norms.

On fluency 80 percent of these children scored above average, and 24 percent ranked in the upper 2 percent on national norms (both significant at .01 level). On flexibility 60 percent were above average, and 8 percent were in the upper two percent (not significant at .01 level but significant at .05 level). On originality 88 percent were above average, and 48 percent were in the upper 2 percent (both significant at .01 level). Thus, the group of socially and emotionally maladjusted children showed unusual strength in fluency and originality but not in flexibility.

A study entiteld "Study of relationship between anxiety and creative thinking," was conducted on Indian population by Arora (1976). Arora conducted the study on a sample of 110 male and 110 female teacher trainees. The study does not take cognizance of the personality dimensions ; nevertheless, the results indicate that for male trainees moderate to normal anxiety appears to be an essential pre-requisite for optimal functioning of creative potential. Arora found a negative correlation between anxiety and creative thinking in the female sample.

Dauw (1965) conducted a more comprehensive study involving high school students as subjects, and using TTCT as the main test. He differentiated between two types of highly creative high school seniors, viz., (1) those scoring high on "originality," and (2) those scoring high on "elaboration." Their characteristics were studied on the basis of their responses to Life Experience Inventory, a self descriptive checklist, and Minnesota Importance Questionnaire (an inventory of vocational needs). All of the high groups were differentiated from the low groups by their total scores on creative personality checklist. In their life-experiences the high "elaborators" tended to be more perfectionist than the high "originators."

Taft and Gilchrist (1970) refer to productivity and creative attitude in their investigations ; and report that students scoring high on both these aspects view themselves as unconventional, willing to take risk, impulsive, observant, imaginative, idealistic, concerned with beauty, having wide range of interests, and subject to emotional conflicts. High scorers on creative productivity alone relate more to lack of self control and neurotic symptoms. They describe themselves as having been unhappy as children, as having received medical attention for nervous or emotional complaints at some stage during their life. In addition, they regard themselves as disorderly, impractical, and lacking in self-control. Thus, those who are actively engaged in artistic and expressional task appear as impractical, disorganized, conflicting both within selves and with their environment. According to the investigator, it provides a strong hint that artistic productivity can be considered as a means of reducing tension caused due to their inner conflicts. On the other hand, high scorers on creative attitude alone correlate positively with the traits of self-actualizing and controlled regressive experiences. They report themselves as intuitive, quick-witted but dependent.

Foster (1971), on the basis of his investigation, concluded that a high creative is sensitive, introvert, tender-minded, conscious and apprehensive.

Some Affective Personality Variable and the Creative Potential

Patel (1977) studied the profiles of creative personality using 16 P.F. and TTCT on 4 components of creative thinking viz., originality, flexibility, fluency, and elaboration. The sample taken comprised 823 high school students—both males and females.

Results of her study indicate that highly fluent males differ from low fluent groups on four personality factors ; and highly flexible on 8 personality factors ; the originators on 3 factors, and elaborators on 7. The highly flexible females were self-sufficient, while those high on B_1 ($\propto$) were dominant and venturesome. Those with a high profile on all creativity variables were venturesome, placid, self-confident, and emotionally stable. Those who were low on all creativity variables were shy.

With a view to determine the effect of dogmatism on creativity, on the one hand, and on intelligence, on the other, Faschinghauer et al. (1977) conducted a study on 30 students as subjects. Rockeach's Dogmatism Scale and scales M-1 through M-4 for G S. Welh's-1975 (Origence and Intellectance typology) on MMPI were administered. Dogmatism correlated 0.44 and 0.30 with scales M-1 and M-3, and −0.33 for M-2 and M-4 respectively. The correlation between dogmatism and intellectance (concrete-abstract) dimension was −0.61, while the correlation between dogmatism and origence was 0.02. Dogmatism, therefore, appears to be related to concrete/abstract dimension of personality.

Rouf (1975) examined the relationship between dogmatism, creativity and complexity. The study indicated a significant negative correlation between dogmatism and creativity. He, thus, corroborated the theory concerning openmindedness and creativity. Dogmatism and creativity were also found to be negatively correlated.

Sex Differences and Sex Identification in Creative Personality

In respect of sex identification and interests, tests of masculinity—femininity of the MMPI have revealed that "highly creative men tend to get high scores on femininity scales and highly creative women, on masculinity scales. Such men are more sensitive than most, and have higher aesthetic interests ; such women are more interested in things and ideas than other women" (Anne Roe, 1963).

Roe (1963) also observed that "the more intellectualized is the male or female, the more likely the person is to get placed on M-F Scales at the opposite poles from most others of the some sex" (p. 136). Roe ascribes it to high degree of sensitivity (an attitude which is regarded as feminine in most cultures) required in scientific and other more intellectual pursuits.

Kogan (1974) writes on sex differences and creativity. He concludes that no such systematic differences are found to occur. However, it is suggested that greater susceptibility of women to distraction related to social context may handicap their creative accomplishment.

The Question of Inheritance and Insanity in Creativity—Survey of Empirical Studies

It would be worth while to review what research studies have offered in respect of the following two points. Such studies are also expected to shed light on the nature of the present problem :

1. The incidence of insanity, emotional conflict and other such sorts of deviant behaviours in the creative person.

2. The role of heredity in creativity.

In respect of the first problem, the evidence collected from the MMPI measures of Berkeley studies points out that "creative groups consistently emerge as having more psychopathology than the more representative members of the same professions" (Barron, 1969, p. 72).

In a less systematic study made by Geortzel and Geortzel (1962), the incidence of psychosis was found to be considerably low in creative persons, although eccentric behaviour and various other forms of behaviour pathology, other than psychosis, were very much common.

Cattell and Butcher (1968), and Drevdahl (1955) found in their empirical studies that eminent researchers were significantly schizothemic (withdrawn), emotionally unstable, self-sufficient and bohemian.

McAllister's (1968) findings clearly show that psychotics deviate strongly from controls on schizothemia and artistic tendencies. The main difference between groups appeared to lie in intelligence, with psychotics, low, and with artists and scientists, high. This finding, according to Eysenck (1976), "accords with the conclusion reached by most workers who examined the traits of creative thinkers, that is, while such persons emerge as unusual individual, they almost always show strong emotional and intellectual controls indicative of integrative personality. Nevertheless, it is of interest that traits on which the creative thinker does appear to deviate from average, are precisely those which, within the range of normal variation, may reflect an increased loading on an underlying personality factor associated with schizophrenia" (Eysenck 1976, p. 32).

Jha quotes study by Drevdahl (1956) who tried to identify the factors of the importance for creativity. Drevdahl took graduates and advanced undergraduate students as his subjects. The tools employed were, Cattell's 16 P.F. questionnaire, Thurstone's PMA Test, and a test selected from Guilford's factor analytic study of creative thinking. The following conclusion was drawn by Drevdahl :

"In terms of these results we might characterize the creative group as somewhat withdrawn and quiescent, more concerned with ideas and things . . . . It appears that suspiciousness and interest in internal mental life, or possibly introceptiveness may be associated with creativity in arts, but that trusting attitude and interest in external things or extroceptiveness may be associated with more creativity in science" (Jha 1978, pp. 84-85).

In respect of the second problem i.e. role of inheritance in creativity, Barron conducted a study at the institute of Medical Genetics in Florence and at the Mental Institute in Rome in 1968-69. The subjects taken were 59 pairs of like-sexed twins : 30 pairs being monozygotic (identical) and 29 pairs were dizygotic (fraternal). The average age was seventeen. Diagnosis of Zygosity was done through medical methods. Instruments used for the study were Gottschaldt figures for adaptive flexibility and Barron-Welsch Art Scale for aesthetic judgement. Inter-class correlations in the identical twins were compared with correlations in the fraternal twins in respect of these two factors. The study indicated the possibility of inheritance of these two factors which are considered important for creativity.

The Berkeley Studies

Evidently, the trend of research studies is definitely in favaur of relating potentiality for creativity to some genetic factors of personality as well as to some other extraneous factors like stress, social pressures, anxiety etc. Numerous studies have been done in diverse fields of creativity—its potential and nurturance. But the most comprehensive study was done at IPAR (Institute of Personality Assessment and Research) at the University of Berkeley which needs a special mention. In this study 530 creative persons representing the fields of writing, architecture, physical science research, engineering, and mathematics were involved as subjects. The creative persons were nominated by experts on the criterion of indisputable creative capacity. Barron (1969) has indicated that the method of study employed was originally not a research method at all. Rather, as the word assessment implies, it was a way of appraising persons. All this was achieved by what is known as "Living-in-Assessment" method.

Barron (1969) points out that inspite of the fact that investigators have employed various different techniques, there appears a consistent agreement in their findings. He suggests that if we take a combination of researches of A.C. Roe, C.W. Taylor, R.B. Cattell, R.D. McCurdy, D.C. Meclelland, B. Edition, J.A. Chambers and H.G. Gough, the following unified picture of the productive scientist can be drawn.

1. High ego strength and stability.
2. Strong need for independence and autonomy, self-sufficiency and self-direction.
3. A high degree of control of impluses.
4. Superior general intelligence.
5. A liking for abstract thinking and drive towards compulsiveness and elegance in explanation.
6. High personal dominance and forcefulness of opinion, but a dislike for personal toned controversy.
7. Rejection of conformity pressures in thinking (although not necessary in social behaviour).
8. Somewhat distant or detached attitude in inter-personal relations, though not without sensitivity or insight ; a preference for dealing with things or abstractions rather than with people.
9. A special interest in some kind of "wagering" which involves pitting oneself against the unknown, so long as one's efforts can be the deciding factor.
10. An excited interest in challenge presented by contradictions, exceptions, and apparent disorder.

MacKinnon (1966), commenting upon Berkeley studies of IPAR, says that these studies have shown that two-thirds or more of each of the creative groups showed a clear tendency towards introversion. He further observed that "whether introvert or extrovert, the creative person is an impressive person, and he is so because he has, to such a large degree, realized his potentialities. Speaking in terms of Jungian functions, MacKinnon has indicated that creative artist shows a preference for feeling ; scientists and engineers, a preference for thinking ; and architects are divided on either of these two. It is also found in these research studies that between perceiving (awareness of something) and judging (coming to conclusion about something) the balance is more tilted towards perception in respect of creative persons.

Barron (1963), R.B. Cattell (1955, 1963) Guilford (1966) had also arrived at similar conclusions.

In the light of the perusal of the empirical studies done so far, the investigator visualized that anxiety as a trait, directly or indirectly seems to be associated with creative potential. And, because all human beings react differently to external stimuli, depending upon the genetic and environmental histories, the investigator attempted to study the relationship between anxiety and creative potential on Indian population in the background of certain other personality dimensions.

CHAPTER IV

The Hypotheses, the Procedure and the Design of the Study

In the light of the theoretical frame work discussed earlier in Chapter II, and also on the basis of the survey of research studies (Chapter III), the investigator cognized certain specific purposes which lead to the present investigation. The purposes of the study, the hypotheses concerning those purposes, the design, and procedure of the study are briefly mentioned here.

THE PURPOSES OF THE STUDY

Primary Purposes

1. To study the relationship, if any, between anxiety at different levels and creative thinking abilities.

2. To study sex differences, if any, on the said relationship of anxiety and creative thinking abilities.

3. To study the relationship, if any, between neuroticism (anxiety-proneness) at its different levels and creative potential.

4. To study sex differences, if any, on the said relationship of neuroticism and creative thinking abilities.

5. To study the interaction of 'E' (extraversion), and 'P' (psychoticism) dimensions of personality and anxiety,

with a view to predict the creative thinking ability of individuals.

6. To study the interaction of 'E' and 'P' dimensions of personality and neuroticism with a view to predict the creative thinking ability of individuals.

7. To compare high and low creatives on anxiety, neuroticism and some other dimensions of personality. (or, to study the personality differences of high and low creatives on anxiety and other dimensions of personality).

8. To compare creative thinking abilities of *hysterics* (persons, high on both extraversion and neuroticism) and *dysthemics* (persons high on neuroticism but low on extraversion).

9. To study sex difference on creative thinking.

Secondary Purposes

10. To study the relationship between anxiety and neuroticism.

11. To verify Eysencks' claim of orthogonality of relationship between the three dimensions of personality (viz., extraversion, neuroticism and psychoticism).

12. To study the nature of distribution of anxiety, psycho-psychotieism, extraversion, and neuroticism in the population.

THE HYPOTHESES OF THE STUDY

Hypotheses Relating to Primary Purposes of the Study

1. To evoke sufficiently creative responses to a stimulus some minimal level of anxiety is essential.

2. There is some optimal level of anxiety which contributes most to evoke creative responses. Further increase in anxiety reduces creative thinking.

3. The relationship between anxiety and creative thinking abilities is curvilinear.

4. The relationship between neuroticism and creative thinking is curvilinear.

5. There is some optimal level of neuroticism which contributes most to evoke creative responses. Further increase in neuroticism does not reduces creative thinking.

6. Extraverts are higher on creative thinking than introverts.

7. Hysterics are higher on creative thinking than dysthemics,

8. Individuals high on psychoticism are less creative than those low on psychoticism.

9. In general, males and females do not differ in regard to their creative thinking abilities.

10. At average to high level of anxiety males are more creative than females.

11. At average to high level of neuroticism males are more creative than females.

12. Anxiety, neuroticism, extraversion, and psychoticism are normally distributed traits.

13. There is positive relationship between anxiety and psychoticism.

14. There is orthogonality of relationship between neuroticism, extraversion, and psychoticism.

15. There is a high, positive relationship between anxiety and neuroticism.

Description of Tools

The present study entitled, "A Study of Relationship between

Anxeity and Creative Potential," has been pursued to include *trait-anxiety* as explicated in different personality organizations. It is commonplace that persons differ in their personality organizations in respect of both their "genotype" and "phenotype." Therefore, trait-anxiety might work differently with different genotypes and phenotypes in respect of their ability to think creatively. In the present study, Eysenck's (1970, 75) concepts of dimensions of personality have been considered whereas to measure trait-anxiety 'Dutt Personality Inventory' (DPI) is used.

The DPI

To measure trait anxiety, DPI (Dutt Personality Inventory Dutt. 1975) was finally chosen for administration to the sample under study. But before the decision was made in favour of the DPI, a test sample of 150 subjects was taken from some of the schools of Delhi who later became a part of the actual sample. The subjects were administered the following four tests : DPI, TMAS, Sinha Anxiety scale, and Spielberger's Trait Anxiety Scale.

Their inter-correlations are reported below :

TABLE 1

DPI	TMAS	SAS	STAS
DPI	0.72	0.82	0.73
TMAS		0.80	0.69
SAS			0.70
STAS			

The Pearson r's mentioned above were found to be statistically significant. On this basis it was decided to use DPI only to measure anxeity. Though any of the above four tests could be employed, DPI was preferred for its Hindi version, multi-component approach and its easy use.

The DPI is a 90-item scale constructed basically to measure anxiety as a characterological trait in an individual.

The scale is based upon some clearly identified components of anxiety ; it avoids the global conceptualization of the term, and utilizes behavioural connotation of the concept.

Following are the psychic components that are utilized in construction of the DPI. In parentheses are mentioned the number of items in the scale.

Insecurity—Loneliness (8) ; Depression (8) ; Inferiority complex (11) ; Guilt-proneness (7) ; Ergic tension (11) ; Paranoid Suspiciousness (10) ; Emotional instability (12) ; Hypochondriac tendencies (8) ; Somatic reactions (10) ; Lie-score (5).

The content and construct validity of the DPI have been established by the author through proper analysis of opinions from experts in the field of anxiety. The relationship with CASQ has been found to be 0.88 (N-350), and with TMAS 0.85 (N=350). This establishes its congruent validity.

The split-half reliability (N=350), corrected by Spearman—Brown formula, has been found to be 0.95

Eysenck Personality Questionnaire (EPQ)

For measurement of dimensions of personality, Eysenck's model of dimensions of personality has been adopted for the simple reason that such a model considers personality as a "more or less stable organization." It does not consider traits as separate entities. Some of the traits tend to exhibit themselves almost always in some personality. This fact is revealed by factor analytic studies conducted by Eysenck and many others. Secondly, the dimensions of personality organizations have been claimed to be completely orthogonal to each other. These are second order factors in factor-analytic terms. Slightly more detailed description of the dimensions of personality has already been made in chapter II (p. 52-54). The three dimensions of personality, according to Eysenck (1960, 1970 & 1975), are *Neuroticism*, *Extraversion*, and *Psychoticism*.

Eysenck Personality Questionnaire (EPQ), which is available in two forms—Junior and Adult—is a development on various personality questionnaires. It differs from the latest of these, that is, the EPI (Eysenck personality Inventory), and includes an additional scale which Eysenck calls Psychoticism scale (P-scale). The first questionnaire in this series was MMQ (Maudsley Medical Questionnaire). MMQ was a forty item measure of neuroticism or emotionality. This was followed by MPI (Maudsley Personality Inventory—Esyenck 1959). MPI was designed to measure Neuroticism and Extraversion. MPI, in turn, was followed by EPI. The EPI was marked from rest of the questionnaires in that it added 'lie-score' to measure dissimulation, the tendency to fake good. Secondly, EPI was also designed to have certain psychometrically desirable improvements over MPI ; for example, the dimensions of Extraversion and Neuroticism were completely independent in EPI, whereas, it was not so in the case of MPI.

The main advantage of the present scale (i.e. EPQ) over others is that it measures an additional dimension 'psychoticism' ('P') of human personality. The term "Psychoticism" simply refers to an underlying personality trait present in varying degrees in all persons. It is only when 'P' is present in extremely marked degrees that a person in later life may be pre-disposed to psychiatric abnormality, especially psychosis. But Eysenck clearly states that such a pre-disposition has nothing to do with actual psychosis ; and only a very small proportion of people with high 'P' scores are likely to develop psychosis in the course of their lives.

In order to avoid psychiatric connotations Eysenck suggests that terms like Neuroticism and Psychoticism may be taken to mean 'emotionality' and 'tough-mindedness' respectively. So, in the present study 'N' and 'P' mean only emotionality and tough mindedness respectively.

In addition to the three dimensions of personality mentioned above, EPQ (Junior) also includes a L-scale (a lie-score scale). Though exact description of the fourth scale has not yet clearly emerged, it, however, may measure dissimulation as well as sociability of an individual. According to Eysenck & Eysenck (1975), motivation for dissimulation depends upon the condition under which the test is administered. Under conditions of high degree of motivation for dissimulation the correlation between Neuroticism and 'L' can be quite high (approx-0.5). But when conditions provide little motivation for dissimulation correlation between Neuroticism and 'L' may vanish all together. Under such conditions there is no sense in using L-scale. It is for this reason, indeed, that L-scale was not used in the present study ; for, neither there was a test-like situation, nor the subjects were going to be personally effected in any way.

The EPQ (Junior) is an eighty one item questionnaire. The scale-wise distribution of items is as follows :

24 items on Extraversion

21 items on Neuroticism

17 items on Psychoticism.

The L-scale comprises the remaining 19 items.

The scanning of items in the EPQ indicates that the questionnaire is more or less culture-fair. Though it is constructed and standardized in England, on a population which has a different cultural background and norms of behaviours, yet, only a few items show a reflection of a particular culture. Almost all of these items tend to demand expressions of emotions that are basically human. Some of the items display subtle shades of differences discernible in by different social groups, but such distinctions can be perceived even within groups in the same society.

However, considering such nuances, some of the items were rephrased and the questionnaire, then, was translated in Hindustani, so that every student could grasp the intent of the statement.

The final version of the translated script was given to the same exploratory sample ; and item analysis was done to ensure statistical normality. With a view to find out reliability of the final version, the two forms were administered to a sample of 75 subjects drawn from TTI Darya Ganj. The time gap between the two administrations of tests was one week. Test-retest reliability was found out to be 0.87, which is highly significant.

Torrance Tests of Creative Thinking (TTCT)

To assess creative potential of the sample of subjects under study Guilford's '*structure of Intellect*' model (Guilford' 1959) was kept in view, a brief out line of which has already been given in Chapter I of this study. In order to obtain scores on the three major components of creativity (viz., originality, flexibility and fluency), as well as scores on the composite ability (creative thinking), it was decided to use TTCT, verbal form A (1974 edition). But before decision to use TTCT was made many theoretical and statistical considerations were carefully examined. The aim was to use the best among the available instruments that are designed to measure creative thinking ability. An illustrative list of such instruments is given below :

Among the many tests standardized abroad, some of the well known measures are :

Guilford's divergent thinking Instruments (Guilford and Merrifield, 1960), Remote Association Tests (Mednick and Mednick, 1964), Ingenius Solutions to Problems Tests (Flanagan, 1958), A.C. Test of Creative Ability (Buhl, 1960), Torrance Tests of Creative Thinking (Torrance, 1966, 1974).

Among those standardized in India, some of the tests are :

Baqer Mehdi's Test of Creative Thinking ; Passi's Test of Creativity ; Creativity Test of Saxena.

Considerations for selecting TTCT were that (i) It has been considered to be one of the best validated and empirically tried out tests both in India as well as abroad.

(ii) It needs no adaptation as has been suggested by Yamamoto (1966). Yamamoto advises that it would be more desirable to keep the tests as they are than adapting them to local situations.

(iii) There are a number of studies which point out that these tests are satisfactory for measuring creative thinking abilities in Indian situation. Such studies are by Raina (1972), Goel (1973), Tanwar (1977), Gakhar and Luthra (1973).

TTCT's are available in four batteries of test activities as under : (i) verbal forms A and B (Form B is an equivalent alternate form to verbal form A) ; (ii) Figural forms A and B.

TTCT Verbal Form A, the one used in the present study, consists of seven activities requiring a total time of 45 minutes in addition to time necessary for giving an orientation, passing out booklets, and giving instructions. The activities are :

(i) *Asking* : "Asking" activity is designed to reveal individuals' ability to sense what one cannot find out from looking at the picture ; and to ask questions that will enable one to fill in the gaps in one's knowledge.

(ii & iii) *Guess causes and Guess consequences* : Both these activities are designed to reveal the subjects' ability to formulate hypotheses concerning cause and effect. They provide one an opportunity to give a picture of his ability to express curiosity ; and to give a picture of one's ability to develop hypotheses.

(iv) *Product Improvement Activity* : It permits the subject to "regress in the service of Ego," and to enable him to play with ideas that he would not dare express in a more serious task.

(v & vi) *"Unusual uses" and "Unusual Questions" Activity* : These activities, adapted from a technique developed by Burkhart (1961), have been included to measure what he terms as "divergent power". According to Burkhart, Divergent power is essential for production of high degree of creative achievement. However, TTCT does not make use of examples in instructions.

(vii) *Just Suppose Activity* : This activity is an adaptation of 'consequences' type test in Guilford's (1959) battery, and is a variation of the "guess" consequences activity of the 'Guess and Ask' series. This variation was designed to elicit a high degree of fantasy. It measures the subject's ability to consider, to evaluate, and to play with unusual ideas, and also to think through their possible consequences.

Scoring of TTCT

All verbal tasks were scored for originality, fluency and flexibility. Elaboration, however, was excluded. According to Torrance (1974), "Those who may like, may score them for elaboration. Until more data are obtained, concerning the verbal elaboration score, most users may prefer not to use this score. Some difficulties have been experienced in obtaining inter-score reliability of high order with beginning scorers." In view of the above statement elaboration scores were not obtained in the present study.

The scoring principles are based on those logical and statistical considerations which have universal applicability. For example, to obtain the fluency score of an activity, one needs to count the total number of relevant responses. Similarly, for flexibility, one is required to count the different categories to which the responses can be put. If there are a number of responses that belong to a single category, only a single flexibility score is to be given for all these responses. The only difficulty (that too not a serious one), which one may encounter, could arise during the assessment for originality. In scoring responses for originality, the principle of statistical infrequency is recommended, i.e., originality is judged primarily by the rarity of responses. Obvious responses, requiring little or no "mental leap" from the stimulus, however, are not considered original inspite of rarity (Torrance, 1974). A response must show some creative strength before it can be considered as original. Torrance set certain norms keeping in view such rare responses. With all these consideration, Torrance, while setting norms, assigned scores of zero to commonplace responses ; score of one to those which showed some creative strength, and were usually given by 5% of the sample ; and a score of two to those responses that showed real creative strength, and were given by 2% or less than 2% of the sample.

THE SAMPLE AND COLLECTION OF DATA

The Sample

For empirical verification of the hypotheses a stratified, random sample of 762 subjects, drawn from 12 senior secondary schools (10+2 pattern), class XI) of the Union Territory of Delhi, was taken. To ensure proper stratification, the schools chosen were such that they represented a rich variety of different types of schools, including the Govt., the Govt. aided and Public-type schools. Schools were further stratified in terms of area of location viz., rural, urban, and slum ; and also in terms of the 'sex' of its student population viz. boys, girls, and co-educational. Every school was randomly selected out of the total population of senior secondary schools in Delhi. For further, randomization, all students of class XI of that school were made the part of sample irrespective of the subject combination they had opted for. In this way the sample was free from any bias in favour of or against a particular course combination—Science, Arts or Commerce groups. Thus, the chosen sample was representative enough to permit optimal generalizability of results.

Collection of Data

Data collection was done in two phases. During the first phase the DPI and EPQ (Junior) were administered on 762 subjects. Data on four personality variables, viz., anxiety, psychoticism, extraversion and neuroticism were obtained. The purpose of gathering data on this fairly large sample was (i) to obtain the univariate statistics, like the mean, median, S D., skewness, etc. ; (ii) to test the orthogonality of the relationship between psychoticism, extraversion, and neuroticism as claimed by Eysenck and Eysenck (1975) ; and (iii) to find out the relationship (Person 'r') between anxiety and neuroticism.

In the second phase, the initial sample of 762 subjects was divided into three groups which constituted the *high anxious*, the *low anxious*, and the *average anxious* groups. This was done on the basis of scores on DPI. The TTCT (Verbal form A) was administered on these three groups of subjects, and thus data on three variables—Originality, flexibility, and fluency —were collected. This final sample consisted of 394 subjects (208 females and 186 males). The reduction in sample occurred due to the simple reason that two separating groups (the slightly high, and the slightly low anxiety groups) were excluded deliberately so that clearly contrasting groups may remain for further analysis of the data Some reduction in data occurred because of experimental mortality also on the second visits to those schools. Thus, the finally selected sample of 394 subjects (both males and femeles) had scores on seven variables. These data were subjected to appropriate statistical analyses.

The Design of the Study

To see whether individuals, at some particular level of anxiety alone or in combination with some level of personality dimensions, e.g. psychoticism and/or extraversion, significantly differ on creative thinking ability, a *complex factorial design* was adopted.

The choice of complex factorial design, especially, was made keeping in view the unique advantage of interaction effects obtainable in this design. The design thus adopted, was of the order 3 × 2 × 2 × 2. Furthermore, it was an *unbalanced factorial design* statistically, because the cell sizes were unequal. To control cell frequencies, so as to make them equal, was logically not possible. Any deliberate attempt to do so would have decreased considerably the reliability of results, for the sub-groups were formed on the basis of external criteria representing systematic biasing from one group to another. One sub-group represented, for example, a highly introverted anxious group, the other sub-group was differently classified. In this design anxiety, the major classification veriable of the study, was considered at 3 levels—high, low, and average. Other classification veriables, viz., P (Psychoticism) and E (Extraversion) were dichotomized, taking median and mean respectively as cut-off points.

The choice of median as cut-off point in the case of 'P' was considered more appopriate statistically as the frequency distribution of P-scores were highly skewed (skewness 9.56 Table 4, P. 94). The 4th veriable taken at two levels was Sex—male and female. For finding F-ratios of main effects for each of the classifying variables, and interaction effects of first, second, and third order, scores on originality, flexibility, and fluency were considered as response variables in turn. Thus, three analyses of variance, in all, were done.

An exactly similar design was adopted with neuroticism as the main classification variable at three levels. The criterion for making three levels in this case was based on quartiles. The three groups of subjects formed were : upper 25% – level 1, lower 25% - level-2 and middle-50%—level III. The response variables in this case too were scores on originality, flexibility, and fluency.

In order to test the hypotheses concerning the personality differences among high and low creatives on variables like anxiety, psychoticism, extraversion, and neuroticism ANOVA was used as the major statistical analysis technique. Taking scores on originality, flexibility, and fluency two contrast groups on each of these variables were made. In order to use ANOVA corresponding scores on anxiety, psychoticism, extraversion and neuroticism were taken as response variable scores, and F-ratios were computed. The groups were :

(i) High and low originals (ii) High and low flexibles (iii) High and low fluent	With anxiety as dependent variable.

These contrast (dichotomous) groups were also compared on psychoticism, extraversion and neuroticism likewise.

Computational work was done at the DUCC (Delhi University Computer Centre).

TERMS AND CONCEPTS, AND THEIR CHARACTERIZATIONS

In main, the terms and concepts used in the present investigation were the following :

(a) (i) Anxiety, (ii) Extraversion, (iii) Psychoticism and, (iv) Neuroticism.

(b) (i) Originality, (ii) Flexibility and, (iii) Fluency.

The two categories of concepts listed above refer to the two aspects of personality of an individual—the affective and the creative. The main purpose/objective of this investigation was to see how the two aspects of personality go together.

Anxiety

For anxiety Dutt's (1975) definition has been taken as operational for the present purpose. Without referring to various theories of anxiety, which mostly attempt at finding out the origin or etiology of anxiety, Dutt (1975) defined anxiety as follows :

"Anxiety constitutes a particular, unpleasant psychological, and physiological reaction of an organism to extrinsic and/or intrinsic threat which amounts to disintegrate or extinct the individual."

Thus, Dutt, like Eysenck and other learning theorists, takes anxiety as conditioned fear and he, basically, does not differentiate between the two, for, their physiological concomitants are the same.

NATURE OF PERSONALITY DIMENSIONS

Eysenck, on the basis of various factor analytic studies, and also on the basis of experimental and theoretical psychology (Eysenck, 1967), evolves a picture of personality that comprises three dimensions : extraversion-introversion, stability-instability (neuroticism or emotionality), and tough-mindedness-tender-mindedness (psychoticism).

Dimensions like extraversion, neuroticisms and psychoticism can operationally be defined in terms of primary factors. On the basis of Eysenck's (1967, 69, 70, 71, 75, 76) studies, the investigator, for the present purpose, defines these dimensions as under.

Extraversion

Extraversion (E), as a dimension of human personality, is a higher order (second order) factor, and is made up of five primary factors—impulsiveness, sociability, liveliness, activity and carefreeness. Persons who score high on all these primary factors are typical extraverts, while those who score low on all these are typical introverts.

Neuroticism

A person with a typical neuroticism (high 'N' score) is an anxious, worring individual, moody and frequently depressed. He is unlikely to sleep well ; and often suffers from various psychosomatic disorders. He is very emotional, reacting too strongly to all sorts of stimuli ; and finds it difficult to get back to normal behaviour after an emotion arousing experience. His strong emotional reactions interfere with his proper adjustments, making him react in irrational ways. When combined with extraversion such an individual is likely to be touchy and restless, to become excitable, and even aggressive. If the higher 'N' individual is to be described in one word one might say that he is a "worrier." His main characteristic is a constant preoccupation with things that might go wrong, and strong emotional reaction of anxiety to these thoughts. The stable individual, on the other hand, tends to respond emotionally slowly and generally weakly ; and tends to return to the neutral base line quickly after an emotional arousal. He is usually calm, even tempered, self possessed, and unworried.

Psychoticism

A person with a typical high 'P' score is defined by Eysenck and Eysenck (1975) as being solitary, not caring for people ; he is often troublesome, not fitting anywhere. He may be cruel and inhumane, lacking in feelings and empathy, and altogether insensitive. He is hostile to others, even to his kith and kin, and aggressive even to the loved ones. He has a liking for odd and unsual things and a disregard for danger. He likes to make fool of other people and tries to upset them. This is a picture of adult high 'P' scorer. The picture of a child who is high on 'P' is quite congruent. He is odd, isolated, troublesome child, glacial and lacking in human feelings for his fellow beings and for animals ; aggressive and hostile even to near and dear ones. He is quite unsocial. Empathy, feeling of guilt, sensitivity to other people are notions that are strange and unfamiliar to such a child.

To define creative potential which comprises originality, flexibility and fluency Torrance's (1974) views have been taken as the base. The operational definitions of these concepts as developed by the investigator are given below :

Originality

It is the capacity of an individual to give responses to a stimulus that are statistically infrequent (rare), showing a mental leap from the stimulus, yet appropriate to it. "A response that may be considered as original must represent some breakaway from the obvious, the commonplace and the banal" (Torrance 1974).

Flexibility

It is the capacity of an individual to use distinct thought categories/approaches in responding to a stimulus.

Fluency

It is the total number of relevant responses given by an individual to a given stimulus. Relevance here is determined in terms of the requirements of the task set forth while introducing the task (stimulus).

Creative Thinking (Creative Potential)

Torrance operationally defines creative thinking as "a process of becoming sensitive to problems, deficiencies, gaps in knowledge, missing elements, disharmonies and so on ; identifying the difficulty, searching for solutions, making guesses or formulating hypotheses about the deficiencies, testing and retesting these hypotheses and possibly modifying and retesting them and finally communating the results" (Torrance 1974). The TTCT itself, used in the present study, is based on the above definition by Torrance

CHAPTER V

Statistical Analysis and Results

The data gathered according to the procedures indicated in Chapter IV, would have remained merely a meaningless heap of facts, without moulding it into a definite shape. To give data the desired shape and direction, they were processed and analysed statistically. Various statistical techniques for analysis of data were selected keeping in view the nature of the data and the purposes of the study. The present chapter, therefore, deals mainly with statistical analyses and the results obtained. The interpretations and the inferences that could logically be drawn, and the recommendations for further studies have been dealt with in the next chapter.

But before the final analyses, relating to purposes of the study and testing the corresponding hypotheses, could be done it was thought necessary to analyse data in relation to some of the secondary purposes. Since the plan of the study was such that the secondary purposes oriented analyses were to lead to primary purposes analyses ; therefore, the data were analysed initially in terms of the secondary purposes of the study. These analyses were conducted on data relating to anxiety, psychoticism, extraversion and neuroticism obtained on 762 subjects who constituted the initial sample of the study. The specific purposes for the analysis of the initial sample were :

(i) To study the nature of distribution of various variables viz., anxiety, psychoticism, extraversion and neuroticism in the population from which the sample was drawn. It was a pre-requisite for further analyses relating to the main problem, because, the choice of statistical techniques to be used depend upon the nature of distribution of scores.

(ii) To study the relationship between anxiety and neuroticism. These two variables are considered to be dependent in someway, and for application of analysis of variance the classification variables should not be mutually dependent, as far as possible.

The statistical analysis of data and results obtained therefrom are presented below. The following notations have been used here : Anxiety (X), Psychoticism (P), Extraversion (E), and Neuroticism (Y).

Univariate Statistics for Anxiety, Psychoticism, Extraversion and Neuroticism

TABLE 2

N (Both Sexes)=762, Average Age=16+

	Mean	S.D	SE_m	Skewness
X	57.17	25.45	0.92	3.61
P	3.08	2.84	0.10	6.34
E	15.66	4.14	0.15	0.21
Y	10.72	4.32	0.17	0.04

TABLE 3

N (Males)=343, Average Age=16+

	Means	S.D.	SE_m	Skewness
X	52.30	21.52	1.16	0.59
P	3.62	2.54	0.14	0.84
E	15.97	3.86	0.21	0.36
Y	9.82	4.14	0.23	0.15

TABLE 4

N (Females)=419, Average age=16+

	Mean	S.D.	SE_m	Skewness
X	61.16	27.64	1.35	4.73
P	2.65	3.00	0.15	9.56
E	15.40	4.33	0.21	0.08
Y	11.45	4.27	0.21	0.06

From the summary of univariate statistics mentioned above in Tables 2 through 4 it is observed that the distribution of 'P' scores deviates significantly from normal distribution, while that of other variables viz. 'X', 'E' and 'Y', does not. The skewness of 'P,' being positive and high, may lead one to conclude that in general people tend to be lower on psychoticism scale.

When males and females were compared with regard to their mean scores on these variables the following results were obtained :

(i) The mean anxiety score of the female group is significantly higher than that of the male group (CR=4.98, significant at .01 level of significance).

(ii) The mean psychoticism score of male group is significantly higher than that of the female group (CR=4.8, significant at .01 level of significance).

(iii) On extraversion, males and females do not differ significantly (CR=.92).

(iv) On Neuroticism, the mean score of the female group is significantly higher than that of the male group (CR=2.74, significant at .01 level of significance).

The above findings, comparing male and female groups on X, Y, E and P, though do not pertain to the main purposes of the study, yet are not redundant. These results confirm the findings of Dutt (1975) and Eysenck (1975), in a way that male and female groups differ on X, Y and P and do not differ on E; thereby, prove the objectivity of the scale. For the sake of analysis of variance the male and female samples can be considered together, for, their distribution is normal except in the case of 'P'.

Rationale for using Skewed 'P' Scores in the Analysis

The significant deviation of 'P' scores from normal distribution, thus, violates the assumption of normality, and also of homogeneity of variance. Apparently, one should not use such skewed data in analysis of variance, because, in the derivation of F-ratios, normality of distribution and homogeniety of variance are assumed to exist. However, according to McNemar (1969 p. 288), there is sufficient evidence that "marked skewness, departures from normal kurtosis and extreme difference in variance do not greatly disrupt the F-test as a basis for judging the significance in analysis of variance. The error introduced by violations of these assumptions is such that F may reach the .05 level about .06 or .07 of the time and the .01 level about .02 of the time. If the investigator wishes to have some assurance that he is not risking the making of the type I error more often than his chosen level of judging significance, he may wish to adopt a somewhat more rigorous level ; requiring a computed F to reach the .01 level provides a very safe base for claiming significance at the .02 level." Such a study is also quoted by Norton in Lindquist. E.F. "Design and Analysis of Experiments, 1963. It is for this reason that skewed 'P' scores have also been considered for analysis of variance.

Study of Orthogonality of Relationthip between Extraversion, Neuroticism and Psychoticism

Eysenck (1975, 1976) extracted the three dimensions of personality factor-analytically as second order factors of personality. He claimed that these three dimensions of personality, viz., Extraversion, Neuroticism, and Psychoticism are orthogonal to each other, i.e., they are independent of each other. To verify the said claim of Eysenck, Pearson r's were computed taking two of the three dimensions of personality at a time. With a view to study the relationship of anxiety with the three dimensions of personality, scores on anxiety were also considered. The correlation matrices showing mutual relationship between these variables are presented below :

TABLE 5

Correlation Matrix

Sample : Male : N-343

	X	P	E	Y
X		0.17	—0.12	0.77
P			0.20	0.13
E				—0.10
Y				

TABLE 6

Sample : Female : N-419

	X	P	E	Y
X		0.56	0.10	0.57
P			0.37	0.12
E				−0.10
Y				

TABLE 7

Total Sample, N=762

	X	P	E	Y
X		0.37	0.00	0.66
P			0.32	0.08
E				−0.11
Y				

All computed 'rs,' mentioned in Tables 5 through 7 were tested for their statistical significance to verify the hopothesis of orthogonality between the three dimensions of personality. The results of the significance of rs are summarised in the Table 8, below :

TABLE 8

Summary Table of Pearson 'rs' with their Significance

Sample	Variable combination	Value of r	Significant/Not Significant at .01 level
Male	E and Y	—0.10	Not significant
N=343	Y and P	0.12	Not significant
	P and E	0.20	Significant
Female	E and Y	0.10	Not significant
N=419	Y and P	00.12	Not significant
	P and E	0.32	Significant
Total	E and Y	−0.10	Not significant
N=762	Y and P	0.08	Not significant
	P and E	0.32	Significant

TABLE 8a

Summary Table—Person rs of anxiety with other Dimensions of Personality, alongwith their Significance at .01 level

Sample	Variable Combination	Value of r	Significant/Not significant
Male	X and P	0.17	Significant
	X and E	—0.12	Not significant
	X and Y	0.77	Significant
Female	X and P	0.56	Significant
	X and E	0.12	Not significant
	X and Y	0.57	Significant
Total	X and P	0.37	Significant
	X and E	0.00	No relationship
	X and Y	0.66	Significant

As is obvious from the Table 8a, the relationship between psychoticism and extraversion is found to be significant. The obtained results, therefore, do not support Eysenck's claim of orthogonality of relationship between these two dimensions i.e., extraversion and psychoticism. The other 'rs' are not found significant statistically.

The relationship between P and X (i.e., psychoticism and anxiety), particularly for the female sample, is quite high. This relationship merits a special consideration, and is, therefore, discussed in Chapter VI.

RESULTS PERTAINING TO FACTORIAL DESIGN, SET 1

Sets of Classifying and Response Variables Defined

Having thus described the initial data in terms of some of

the secondary objectives mentioned in Chapter IV, the investigator analysed the final sample for obtaining results relating to the main study.

According to the proposed design, which is a complex unbalanced factorial design of the order $3\times2\times2\times2$, the data were treated under GLM (General Linear Model) procedures of SAS (Statistical Analysis System). The justification for subjecting the data to GLM procedures for analysis of variance was that these procedures are quite comprehensive to treat data more effectively, especially when the experimental design is unbalanced (i.e., cell frequencies are unequal or disproportional).

The analysis of variance of the factorial design used was done in two sets of classifying variables. The first set of variables was constituted by classifying 'X' (at three levels), P (at two levels), E (at two levels) and Sex (male and female). In the second set 'X' (anxiety) was replaced by 'Y' (Neuroticism) while P, E and Sex were retained as they were in the first set. In the two sets of variables the response variables were (i) originality, (ii) Flexibility, and (iii) Fluency.

The different levels of the classifying variables were given the following notations for the convenience of the computer system :

Anxiety (ANX, X)—High (level 1), Average (level 2), and Low (level 3).

Psychoticism (PSYCHOT, P)—High (level 1), and Low (level 2).

Extraversion (EXTRA, E) High (level 1), and Low (level 2).

Neuroticism (NEUROT, Y)—High (level 1), Average (level 2), and Low (level 3).

Sex—Female (level 1), Male (level 2).

The response variables were given the notations : Originality (ORIGIN), Flexibility (FLEX), Fluency (FLUN).

Originality as Response Variable

Analysis of the factorial design (Set 1) was carried out using GLM procedure ; and the obtained results are presented alongwith the summary of variance, F-ratios and their probabilities of being greater than the critical values for each of the main effects, as well as for all possible interactions. Table 9 pertains to results with originality as response variable.

TABLE 9

General Linear Model Procedures

Dependent Variable : Origin

Source	DF	SS	Mean Square	F-value	PR>F
Model	23	5839.42	258.24	2.91	0.0001
Error	370	32789.52	88.60		STD. DEV
Corrected Total	393	38728.93			9.41
X	2	907.4414		5.12	0.0064
P	1	1076.29		12.15	0.0006
E	1	420.97		4.75	0.0299
Sex	1	173.78		2.07	0.1507
X*P	2	137.36		0.77	0.4615
X*E	2	146.19		0.82	0.4391
X* Sex	2	4.111		0.02	0.9771
P*E	1	3.99		0 05	0.8321
P* Sex	1	15.22		0.17	0.6788
E* Sex	1	63.39		0.71	0 3984
X*P*E	2	676.90		3.82	0.0228
X*P* Sex	2	481.03		2.71	0.0676
P*E* Sex	1	155.08		1.75	0.1867
X*E* Sex	2	17.09		0.10	0.9081
X*P*E* Sex	2	347.83		1.96	0.1428

A perusal of the results shown in Table 9 reveals that the following F-ratios are significant :

A. Main Effects

(i) Classifying variables—'X' : F=5.12
df = 2/370 ; Significant at .0064 level of significance.

(ii) Classifying variables—'P' : F=12.15
df=1/370 : Significant at .03 level of significance.

(iii) Classifying variable—'E' : F=4.75
df=1/370 ; Significant at 0.3 level of Significance.

With a view to find out as to which of the different levels of the classifying variables differ significantly from others with respect to scores on originality, Duncan's Multiple G.C. Range Test was applied. It may be noted here that Duncan's Multiple Group Comparison Range test is considered one of the best and most widely used tests to determine the significance of differences between pairs of means or LS Means (Least Square Means). It is a valid substitute for t-ratio test, and is applicable especially to groups that are not independently/randomly drawn from the population, but represent some 'systematic biasing' in their formation. The application of t-test in such cases is not statistically sound (Senter, 1976, p. 284).

The results of Duncan's Multiple Range Test, for multiple group comparisons are given in Table 9(a) through 9(d). The test could be applid conveniently on main effects only.

Looking into the results it is obious that :

(i) Level 1 and level 2 of variable 'X' do not differ significantly in respect of their mean originality scores.

(ii) Level 1 of 'X' differs significantly from Level 3.

(iii) Level 2 of 'X' differs significantly from Level 3.

The mean originality score at level 3 of 'X' is lowest (Mean = 47.38).

The second significant F was found in the case of 'P' (Psychoticism) which is significant at .0006 level of significance. When Duncan's test was applied to it (Table 9b), it was found that mean originality score at level 2 (the lower level of 'P') is significantly higher than mean originality score at level 1 (the higher level).

TABLE 9a

Duncan's Multiple Range Test for Variable Origin

(Means with the same letter are not significantly different)

Alpha Level =.05	DF=370	MS=88.6203	
Grouping	Mean	N	X
A	50.7475	103	1
A	50.4591	196	2
A	47.3789	95	3

TABLE 9b

Duncan's Multiple Range Test for Variable Origin

(Means with the same letter are not significantly different)

Alpha Level=.05	DF=370	MS=89.6203	
Grouping	Mean	N	P
A	51.0954	241	2
B	47.7385	153	1

TABLE 9c

Duncan's Multiple Range Test for Variabe Origin

(Means with the same letter are not significantly different)

Alpha Level=.05	DF=370	MS=88.6253	
Grouping	Mean	N	E
A	50.6173	196	1
A	48.9747	198	2

TABLE 9d

Duncan's Multiple Range Test for Variable Origin

(Means with the same letter are not significantly different)

Alpha Level=.05 DF=370 MS=88.6203

Grouping	Mean	N	Sex
A	50.5987	186	M
A	49.3721	208	F

A perusal of results of 'E' as classifying variable Tables 9 and 9c) indicates the absence of clear-cut results for direct generalizations. According to F ratio (F=4.75, df=1/370 significant at .026 level) the two levels of E should differ significantly from each other, in respect of their mean originality scores. But the results of Duncan's Test do not indicate any significant difference even at .05 level of significance. According to Senter (1976, p. 291), while doing the analysis of variance one is occasionally, though not often, faced with such a situation. He recommends that in such a case the results of Duncan's test should guide statistical analysis and interpretation.

In the light of this discussion, therefore, it is held that the extraversion dimension cannot be treated as a significant factor to evoke creative (original) responses.

In the case of "sex" as a classifying variable there is no significant F. Clearly sex, as male or female, cannot be treated as a factor influencing/determining originality of responses.

The only significant interaction in the results of analysis of variance presented in Table 9 is X*P*E (F=3.82, df=2/370, significant at .023 level). It means that a unique combination of certain levels of these variables gives the best *response surface* for originality. To find out that unique combination of the levels of variables in this interaction, LS Means (Least Square Means) were computed. A perusal of these LS Means indicates that level combination 1.2.1 respectively gives highest means score on originality (Mean=60.26, SEM=2.3). On the other hand, level combination 3, 1, 2 gives the least mean originality score (Mean=42.00, SEM=5.25). We can safely infer from these results that :

(i) High level of anxiety, low level of psychoticism and high level of Extraversion, when present simultaneously in individuals, may trigger off many more original responses.

TABLE 10

General Linear Models Procedures

Dependent Variable : Flex

Source	DF	S.S.	Mean Square	F. value	PR>F
Model	23	6645.21	288.92	3.28	0.0001
Error	370	32640.88	88.22		STD DEV
Corrected Total	393	39286.08			9.39
X	2	557.20		3.16	0.0437
P	1	1744.35		19.77	0.0001
E	1	516.57		5.86	0.0160
Sex	1	436.48		4.95	0.0267
X*P	2	65.02		0.37	0.6920
X*E	2	44.54		0.25	0.7770
X* Sex	2	45.54		0.26	0.7727
P*E	1	16.32		0.19	0.6673
P* Sex	1	24.77		0.28	0.5965
E* Sex	1	8.57		0.10	0.5754
X*P*E	2	971.84		5.51	0.0044
X*P* Sex	2	389.37		2.21	0.1115
P*E* Sex	1	231.14		2.62	0.1064
X*E* Sex	2	71.51		0.41	0.6671
X*P*E* Sex	2	201.47		1.14	0.3203

(ii) A combination of low level of anxiety, high level of psychoticism and low level of extraversion tends to limit the original responses.

Flexibility as Response Variable

The second analysis of variance in this set was done with 'FLEX' as response variable. The results are presented in Table 10 (P. 104) and in Tables 10a through 10d.

From the results of this analysis of variance presented in Table 10, it is observed that the F-ratios for all the four main effects are significant. The F-ratios are :

TABLE 10a

General Linear Models Procedure

Duncan's Multiple Range Test for Variable Flex

(Means with the same letter are not significantly different)

Alpha Level=.05 DF=370 MS=88.2186

Grouping	Mean	N	X
A	50.4183	196	2
A	50.1165	103	1
A	48.810526	95	3

TABLE 10b

General Linear Models Procedure
Duncan's Multiple Range Test for Variable Flex

(Means with the same letter are not significantly different)

Alpha Level=.05 DF=370 MS=FB 88.2186

Grouping	Mean	N	P
A	51.6224	241	2
B	47.3202	153	1

TABLE 10c

General Linear Models Procedure
Duncan's Multiple Range Test for Variable Flex

(Means with the same letter are not significantly different)

Alpha Level=.05 DF=370 MS=88.2186

Grouping	Mean	N	E
A	51.0204	196	1
B	48.8939	198	2

TABLE 10d

General Linear Models Procedure
Duncan's Multiple Range Test for Variable Flex

(Means with the same letter are not significantly different)

Alpha Level=.05 DF=370 MS=88.2186

Grouping	Means	N	SEX
A	51.4677	186	M
B	48.5961	208	F

(i) Classifying variable : X, F=3.16, df=2/370, significant at .04 level of significance.

(ii) Classifying variable : 'P', F=19.77, df=1/370, significant at .0001 level of significance.

(iii) Classifying variable : 'E', F=5.86, df=1/370, significant at .016 level of significance.

(iv) Variable Sex : F=4.95, df=1/370, significant at .03 level of significance.

However, the results of the Duncan's test (Table 10a), in the case of 'X' as classifying variable, indicate that the three levels of 'X' do not differ significantly from one another even at .05 level of signifiance. Taking these results as final for the present study, it implies that for flexibility as component of creative thinking, anxiety is not a factor at all. Whatever the differences in the mean flexibility score at the three levels of 'X' they can be attributed to mere chance.

In the case of variable 'P', the mean flexibility score at lower level is significantly higher than that at high level (Table 10b).

In the case of variable 'E', the mean flexibility score at high level (level 1) is significantly higher than that at lower level (Table 10c).

On the 'Sex' variable, males are found to be more flexible than females (Table 10d).

In regard to interaction effects of this analysis the same second order interaction (i.e. X*P*E), was found significant as in the case of originality. X*P*E reveal a high F-ratio (F=5.51, df=2/370) significant at .0044 level of significance (Table 10).

Looking into the LS Means computed for this interaction, level combination 1, 2, 1 is the most effective (Mean=60.26, SEM=2.32) while level combination 3, 1, 2 is the least effective (M=42.00, SEM=5.25) in terms of high flexibility scores. It implies that individuals who are high on anxiety, low on psychoticism and high on extraversion tend to be highly flexible in their verbal behaviour. Low level of anxiety, high level of psychoticism and low level of extraversion when present simultaneously in individuals, tend to limit their verbal flexibility scores.

Fluency as Response Variable

Results of the third alalysis of variance with fluency as the response variable are presented in Table 11 and Tables 11a through 11d.

The results in Table 11 indicate three significant Fs for main effects. None of the interaction effects is significant. The significant main effects are :

TABLE 11

General Linear Modes Procedures

Dependent Variable : Flun

Source	DF	S.S.	Mean Square	F. value	PR>F
Model	23	5942.28	258.66	2.86	0.0001
Error	370	35519.74	96.59		STD DEV
Correct Total	393	39465.			9.51
X	2	462.69		2.66	0.0710
P	1	1267.74		13.99	0.0002
E	1	664.69		7.34	0.0071
Sex	1	895.82		9.89	0.0018
X*P	2	8.59		0.05	0.9537
X*E	2	8.76		0.05	0.9528
X* Sex	2	23.19		0.13	0.8789
P*E	1	1.5		0.02	0.8975
P* Sex	1	0.005		0.00	0.9941
E* Sex	1	0.035		0.00	0.9844
X*P*E	2	451.59		2.49	0.0841
X*P* Sex	2	280.59		2.55	0 2139
P*E* Sex	1	177.24		1.96	0.1627
X*E* Sex	2	5.05		0.03	3.9725
X*P*E* Sex	2	160 59		0.89	0.4130

(i) Variable P : F=13.99, df 1/370; significant at .0002 level.

(ii) Variable E : F=7.34, df=1/370 significant at .007 level.

(iii) Variable Sex : F=9.89, df=1/370 significant at .0018 level.

All the three main effects are highly significant.

Looking into the results of the Duncan's test (Tables presented below) for finding the significance of the difference of means, it is evident that :

(i) Level 2 (low level) of Psychoticism is significantly more contributory than level 1 (high level).

(ii) Extraverts are more fluent than introverts.

(iii) Males are more fluent than females.

No interaction with 'X' was found significant in the case of fluency as response variable.

TABLE 11a

General Linear Models Procedure

Duncan's Multiple Range Test for Variable Flun

(Means with the same letter are not significantly different)

Alpha Level=.05 DF=370 MS=90.5939

Grouping	Mean	N	X
A	50.6530	196	2
A	49.9417	103	1
A	48.7263	95	3

TABLE 11b

General Linear Models Procedure

Duncan's Multiple Range Test for Variance Flun

(Means with the same letter are not significantly different)

Alpha Level=.05 DF=370 MS—90.5939

Grouping	Mean	N	P
A	31.2572	241	2
B	48.5261	153	1

TABLE 11c

General Linear Models Procedure
Duncan's Multiple Range Test for Variable Flun

(Means with the same letter are not significantly different)

Alpha Level=.05 DF=370 MS=90.5939

Grouping	Mean	N	E
A	51.2857	196	1
B	48.7323	198	2

TABLE 11d

General Linear Models Procedure
Duncan's Multiple Range Test for Variable Flun

(Means with the same letter are not significantly different)

Alpha Level=.05 DF=370 MS=90.5939

Grouping	Mean	N	SEX
A	52.0215	186	M
B	48.1971	208	F

ANALYSES OF VARIANCE WITH NEUROTICISM AS MAIN CLASSIFYING VARIABLE

(The Second set of Analyses)

The second set of analyses was done by replacing anxiety with neuroticism from earlier set of classifying variables. The second set, thus became Y, P, E, and Sex, where Y stands for neuroticism, P, E and Sex retain the same connotations as they had in the earlier set. The reason for replacing 'X' with Y were that :

The Pearson 'r' between 'X' and 'Y' being 0.66 (Table 7) indicates that though the relationship between the two variables is quite high yet they do not stand for identical traits.

Anxiety is assumed to be "phenotype" and neuroticism its "genotype." Neuroticism can be taken as anxiety-proneness.

The design of the experiment for analysis of variance of this set is identical with that of the anxiety set. In presenting the results of this set, main effects of 'Y' and interaction effects involving 'Y' as one of the variables have been considered. Other main effects i.e., of P, E and Sex have already been dealt with. Interaction effects not involving Y are not relevant to the present study ; hence these have not been considered.

Originality as Response Variable

The results of this analysis are presented in Table 12 and 12a (p. 112-113).

Looking into Table 12, one finds that 'Y' constitutes a significant F, (F=18.77, df=2/370 significant at .0001 level).

Now looking into Table 12a, it is observed that for all the three levels of Y (i.e., 1, 2, 3) their mean originality scores differ significantly among themselves. The mean score at level 1 being the highest and at level 3—the lowest. The means at level 1, 2 and 3 are 53.75, 49,16 and 45.95 respectively.

The following interactions with Y are found to be significant.

(i) Y*E ; F=8.60, df=2/370, Significant at .0002 level.

(ii) Y* Sex ; F=5.32, df=2/370, Significant at .0053 level.

(iii) Y*P*E* Sex ; F=4.43, df=2/370, Significant at .0125 level of significance.

To interpret these significant interactions the LS Means of different level combinations were computed and used here for interpretation of results.

Looking into these means following information is obtained.

In interaction (i), Y*E, the highest scoring group is constituted by level combination 1, 1 i.e., persons high both on extraversion and neuroticism score high on originality.

In interaction (ii), Y* Sex, the LS Means show that males high on neuroticism score significantly higher than females.

TABLE 12

General Linear Model Procedure

Dependent Variable ; Origin.

Source	DF	Sum of squares	Mean square	F. value	PR>F
Model	23	9944.73	432.38	5.56	0.0001
Error	370	28784.20	77.80		STD DEV
Corrected Total	393	38628.93			8.82
Y	2	2920.57		18.77	0.0001
P	1	864.23		11.11	0.0009
E	1	276.57		3.56	0.0601
Sex	1	7.37		0.09	0.7585
Y*P	2	214.40		1.38	0.2534
Y*E	2	1338.22		8.60	0.0002
Y* Sex	2	827.07		5.32	0.0053
P*E	1	25.74		0.33	0.5654
P* Sex	1	32.30		0.42	0.5192
E* Sex	1	42.01		0.54	0.4629
Y*P*E	2	365.45		2.35	0.0968
Y*P* Sex	2	250.75		1.61	0.2110
P*E* Sex	1	722.22		9.28	0.0025
Y*E* Sex	2	128.41		0.81	0.4445
Y*P*E* Sex	2	689.96		4.43	0.0125

TABLE 12a

General Linear Models Procedure
Duncan's Multiple Range Test for Variable Origin

(Means with the same letter are not significantly different)

Alpha Level=.05 DF=370 MS=77.7951

Grouping	Mean	N	Y
A	53.7476	107	1
B	49.1556	212	2
C	45.9466	75	3

When males and females were compared in respect of their mean originality scores at different levels of neuroticism, males are found to score significantly higher than females, but only at average level of neuroticism. The C.R. at this level is 3.36, which is significant at .01 level.

In the third order interaction (four factor interaction) Y*P*E* Sex the highest scoring level combination is 1.2.1.F (LS Means=66 SEM=2.45). The least scoring group is constituted by level combination 3.2.1. M (LS Means 35, SEM=4.41).

Flexibility as Response Variable

The results of this analysis of variance are presented in Tables 13 and 13a.

From Table 13, it is clear that 'Y' constitutes a significant F with flexibility as response variable. The obtained F=16.87 (df=2/370), is significant at .0001 level.

The results of Duncan's test, presented in Table 13a show that mean flexibility scores at the three levels of Y are significantly different from one another, in such a manner that individuals at high level of 'Y' are low on flexibility.

The following interactions of 'Y' with other personality variables were found significant :

(i) Y*E with F=7.04, df=2/370, significant at .0001 level.

(ii) Y*Sex with F=3.50, df=2/370, significant at .03 level.

(iii) Y*P*E with F=5.13, df=2/370, significant at .006 level.

The table of LS Means of interactions further yielded the following information regarding significant interactions :

(a) The most contributory level combination to evoke flexible responses comprises high level of neuroticism and high level of extraversion (LS Mean=58.03, SEM=1.35). The least contributory level combination of extraversion with neuroticism is low level of neuroticism coupled with low level of extraversion (LS Means=42.79, SEM=2.53).

(b) In the case of Y*SEX, the table of LS Means showed that males with high level of neuroticism are the highest scorers on flexibility (LS Mean=54.51, SEM=1.34). The least scoring group in this interaction is constituted by Males with low level of neuroticism (LS Mean 43.14, SEM=1.59).

In the second order significant interaction viz. Y*P*E, the most contributory level combination is constituted by individuals high on neuroticism, low on psychoticism, and high on extraversion (LS Mean of this particular interaction is 64 98, SEM=1 95). The least scoring group in this interaction is constituted by low scores on neuroticism high scores on psychoticism and low scores on extraversion (LS Mean=38.13. SEM=4.86).

TABLE 13

General Linear Models Procedure

Dependent Variable : Flex

Source	DF	Sum of Squares	Mean Square	F-Value	PR>F
Model	23	11262.92	489.69	6.47	0.0001
Error	370	28023.16	75.74		STD DEV
Total	393	39286.09			8.70
Y	2	2556.07			0.0001
P	1	2168.51		28.64	0.0001
E	1	650.06		8.72	0.0034
Sex	1	216.13		2.85	0.0923
Y*P	2	175.12		1.16	0.3168
Y*E	2	1066.08		7.04	0.0010
Y* Sex	2	529.90		3.50	0.0318
P*E	1	1.33		0.02	0.8944
P* Sex	1	3.50		0.05	0.8283
E* Sex	1	15.08		0.20	0.6557
Y*P*E	2	776.37		5.13	0.0264
Y*P* Sex	2	136.58		0.80	0.4158
P*E* Sex	1	430.46		5.68	0.0176
Y*E* Sex	2	39.49		0.26	0.7106
Y*P*E* Sex	2	370.82		2.45	0.0879

TABLE 13A

General Linear Models Procedure

Duncan's Multiple Range Test for Variable Flex

(Means with the same letter are not significantly different)

Alpha Level=.05 DF=370 MS=75.7383

Grouping	Mean	N	Y
A	52.8317	107	1
B	49.9339	212	2
C	45.8933	75	3

Fluency as Response Variable

The results of this analysis of variance are presented in Tables 14 and 14a.

Results presented in Table 14 clearly show that 'Y' constitutes a significant F=ratio, (F-16.32, df=2/370 ; significant at .0001 level),

The results of Duncan's test present in Table 14a further reveal that mean fluency scores at the three levels of 'Y' differ significantly from one another in such a manner that individuals high on neuroticism are also high on fluency, and individuals low on neuroticism are low on fluency.

Regarding interaction effects of other personality variables with Y, it is clear that there are only two such significant interactions, which are mentioned as under :

(i) Y*E, with F=4.83, df=2/370 Significant at 00.85 level.

(ii) Y*P*E*Sex, with F=4.83, df=2/370 Significant at .0085 level.

The table of LS Means of interaction Y*P*E*Sex yields the following additional information in regard to these interactions:

(a) In the case of first order interaction Y*E, the most contributory level combination to evoke fluent responses is 1.1 i.e., an interaction of high level of neuroticism and high level of extraversion yields most fluent responses (LS Mean=57.96, SEM=1.38).

(b) On the other hand, the least contributory level combination of this interaction is 3.2 i.e., an interaction of low level of neuroticism and low level of extraversion end to limit fluency of responses (LS Mean=42.79, SEM=2.53)

TABLE 14

General Linear Models Procedure

Dependent Variable : Flun

Source	DF	Sum of Square	Mean Square	F-value	PR>F
Model	23	10150.77	441.34	5.57	0.0001
Error	370	29316.23	79.24		STD DEV
Corrected Total	393	39468.99			8.0001
Y	2	2586.68		16.32	0.0002
P	1	1523.91		19.23	0 0001
E	1	817.82		10.32	0.0014
Sex	1	559.20		7.06	0.0082
Y*P	2	105.26		0.68	0.5163
Y*E	2	765.42		5.83	0.0085
Y* Sex	2	158.46		1.00	0.3689
P*E	1	57.79		0.69	0.4062
P* Sex	1	23.09		0.29	0.5817
E* Sex	1	5.25		0.07	0.7862
Y*P*E	2	276.74		1.75	0.1759
Y*P* Sex	2	71.68		0.45	0.6365
P*E* Sex	1	243.47		6.86	0.0092
Y*E* Sex	2	1.30		0.01	0.9917
Y*P*E* Sex	2	764.94		4.83	0.0085

TABLE 14a

General Linear Models Procedure

Duncan's Multiple Range Test for Variable Flun

(Means with the same letter are not significantly different)

Alpha Level=.05 DF=370 MS=73.2385

Grouping	Mean	N	Y
A	5288.78	107	1
B	49.7405	212	2
C	46.6266	75	3

Investigating Curvilinearity of Relationship

The pearson "rs" of neuroticism with originality, flexibility and fluency were found to be 0.26, 0.24 and 0.21 respectively. All these correlations of neuroticism with each of the creative thinking abilities are found to be significant, but are low. The low Pearson 'rs' cast some doubt whether the relationship in question can be represented through linear regression of creative thinking abilities on neuroticism (i.e., anxiety-proneness). The regression, if it is not linear, may be represented through a curve. The curvilinearity of relationship can be established, if at all, one is able to reject the hypothesis of linearity of regression. And according to McNemar (1969, pp. 314, 317) the hypothesis of linearity of regression can be rejected if the departure of array means from linear regression falls beyond .01 level of significance. When this happens, it follows that correlation coefficients and linear regressions are not the appropriate measures to describe the relationship. McNemar (op. cit. p. 317) further remarks that "the test of linearity can lead to definite conclusion that the regression is curvilinear (if F is large enough)." For computation of correlation ratio (η) and for testing its significance, one can compute Fs of linear regression. "It is seen that for fixed dfs the value of F, even though computed from sums rather than their equivalents in terms of η^2, can be thought of as depending upon the size of η^2. Therefore, a significant F indicates at significant correlation ratio" (McNemar, 1969, p. 308).

With these statistical considerations F-ratio of linear regressions of the creative thinking abilities on neuroticism were computed. The results of such regressions and their corresponding Fs are presented in Tables 15 through 17.

From these tables it is obvious that :

(i) With originality as response variable and neuroticism as independent variable, the F is 37.26 which is highly significant at .0001 level.

TABLE 15

General Linear Models Procedure

Dependent Variable : Origin

Source	DF	Sum of Squares	Mean Squares	F-value	PR>F
Model	4	5826.11	1456.70	17.22	0.0001
Error	389	32909.13	84.58		
Corrected Total	393	38726.93			
Anxiety	1	241.76		2.86	0.0817
Psychot	1	3202.48		27.22	0.0001
Extra	1	532.37		6.29	0.3225
Neurot	1	3151.76		37.26	0.0001

TABLE 16

General Linear Model Procedures

Dependent Variable : Flex

Source	DF	Sum of Squares	Mean Squares	F-value	PR>F
Model	4	6272.14	2568.04	18.48	0.0001
Error	389	33013.54	84.87	STD Dev.	
Corrected Total	393	39286.08		9.21	
Anxiety	1	593.80		7.00	0.0085
Psychot	1	2452.90		28.90	0.0001
Extra	1	861.85		10.16	0.0016
Neurot	1	3548.08		41.86	0.0001

TABLE 17

General Linear Model Procedures

Dependent Variable : Flun

Source	DF	Sum of Squares	Mean Squares	F-value	PR>F
Model	4	4800 61	1200.45	13.47	0.0001
Error	389	34686.39	89.12		STD DEV
Corrected Total	393	39469.00			8.44
Anxiety	1	849.93		9.54	0.0022
Psychot	1	1273.56		14.29	0.0002
Extra	1	695.03		7.80	0.0055
Neurot	1	2255.23		36.53	0.0001

Thus the hypothesis of linearity is rejected and curvilinearity of relaltionship between originality and neuroticism is established.

(ii) In Table 16, with flexibility as the dependent variable and neuroticism as the independent variable, the F-ratio is 41.86, significant at .0001 level.

The hypothesis of linearity of relationship between flexibility and neuroticism, therefore, stands rejected in this case too.

(iii) Similarly with fluency as dependent variable and neuroticism as independent variable, the F-ratio is 36.53 which is significant at .0001 level. (Table 17).

Thus, the hypothesis of linearity of relationship between fluency and neuroticism also stands rejected.

In the present design the investigator considered the regression of creative thinking on neuroticism only, for examining the curvilinearity of relationship. The curvilinearity of anxiety, however could not be examined, because the scores of anxiety were truncated in the present design. Further non-linear regression curves were drawn to observe the nature of relationship between neuroticism and creative thinking which were found consistent with statistical results. The conclusions thus are corroborated.

Contrast Groups of Creatives Compared on Anxiety and other Personality Dimensions

The objective behind this analysis was to study whether high and low creatives differ on anxiety, neuroticism, and on some other personality variables or not. No doubt, indirect inference to this effect could be drawn on the basis of analysis of variance of the factorial design, but such an indirect inference may not be true logically. For example, if 'A' implies 'B' it is logically not necessary that 'B' implies A as well. In other words one may hold that inference from factorial design could constitute only a hypothesis, while direct comparision of such contrast groups is a direct empirical verification.

From the earlier analysis, it is observed that the high and average anxious groups are superior to the low anxious group on creative thinking abilities. The question is : 'Do the high and low creatives also differ on anxiety' ? To answer this question, a design was made ; Such a design would add to the comprehension of the present study.

In this design two contrast groups on each of the creative thinking abililties were constituted on the basis of Q 1 and Q 3 as cut-off points. That is, the first quartile constituted the low creative group, while the fourth quartile constituted the high creative group in respect of each of the creative thinking abilities. To analyse the data, simple analysis of variance (ANOVA) procedures were applied. The relative status of

TABLE 18

Analysis of Variance Procedure

Class Level Information

Class	Levels	Values
0	2	1, 2

Number of Observations in Data Set=394

Dependent Variable : ANX

Source	DF	Sum of Squares	Mean Square	F Value	PR>F	R. Square	C.V.
Model	1	2497.28	2497.28	4.05	0.0455	0.02	40.5751
Error	216	133295.55	6170.11		STD DEV		ANX Mean
Corrected Total	217	133792.83			24.843		61.07

Source	DF	Anova SS	F Value	PR>F
0	1	2497 2780/287	4 05	0.0455

Dependent Variable : Psychot

Source	DF	Sum of Squares	Mean Squares	F Value	PR>F	R. Square	C.V.
Model	1	70.86	70.86	13.56	0.0003	0.06	71.29
Error	216	1128.85	5.23		STD DEV		Psychot Mean
Corrected Total	217	1199.71			2.29		3.21

Source	DF	Anova SS	F Value	PR>F
0	1	70 85740405	13.56	0.0003

Table 18 (Contd.)

Dependent Variable : Extra

Source	DF	Sum of Squares	Mean Square	F Value	PR>F	R. Square	C.V.
Model		10.66	10.67	0.62	0.4327	0 002863	26.57
Error	216	3727.98	17.26		STD DEV		Extra Mean
C rrected Total	217	3730.64			4 15		15.63

Source	DF	Anova SS	F Value	PR>F
0	1	10.66595526	0.62	0.4327

Dependent Variable : Neurot

Source	DF	Sum of Squares	Mean Square	F Value	PR>F	R. Square	C.V.
Model	1	401.12	401.12	21.81	0.0001	0.09	35.05
Error	216	3971.95	19.38		STD DEV		Neurot Mean
Corrected Total	217	4377.06000734			4.28		12.23

Source	DF	Anova SS	F Value	PR>F
0	1	401.12	21.01	0.0001

0	N	ANX	Psychot	Extra	Neurot
1	112	66.37	2.65	75.24	13.35
2	106	57.59	3.79	13.40	10.84

TABLE 19

Analysis of Variance Procedure

Class Level Information

Class	Levels	Values
'F'	2	1, 2

Number of Observations in Data Set=394

Analysis of Variance Procedure

Dependent Variable : ANX

Source	DF	Sum of Squares	Mean Square	F Value	PR>F	R. Square	C.V.
Model	1	251.56	257.54	0.44	0.59	0.0019	39.36
Error	227	170790.43	576.17		STD DEV		ANX Mean
Corrected Total	229	131041.98			24.00		60.99

Source	DF	Anova SS	F Value	PR>F
F	1	251.55	0.44	0.5094

Dependent Variable : Psychot

Source	DF	Sum of Squares	Mean Square	F Value	PR>F	R. Square	C.V
Model	1	51.69	51.69	10.18	0.0016	0.04	69.45
Error	227	1152.61	6.08		STD DEV		Psychot Mean
Corrected Total	228	1204.31			2.25		3.24

Source	DF	Anova SS	F Value	PR>F
F	1	51.694	10.18	0.0016

Table 19 (Contd.)

Dependent Variable : Extra

Source	DF	Sum of Squares	Mean Square	F Value	PR>F	R. Square	C.V.
Model	1	50.70	50.70361695	2.72	0.1007	0.0118	27.79
Error	227	4236.06	18.66107904		STD DEV		Extra Mean
Corrected Total	228	4236.77			4.32		15.55

Source	DF	Anova SS	F Value	PR>F
F	1	50.76361595	2.72	0.1007

Dependent Variable : Neurot

Source	DF	Sum of Squares	Mean Square	F Value	PR>F	R. Square	C.V.
Model	1	379.25	379.25	21.17	0.0001	0.08	35.49
Error	227	4066.49	37.91		STD DEV		Neurot Mean
Corrected Total	228	4445.74			4.23		11.93

Source	DF	Anova SS	F Value	PR>F
F	1	379.25	21.17	0.0001

TABLE 20

Analysis of Variance Procedure

Class	Levels	Values
FL	2	1, 2

Number of Observations in Data Set=394

Dependent Variable : ANX

Source	DF	Sum of Squares	Mean Square	F Value	PR>F	R. Square	C.V.
Model	1	67.62	67.62	0.11	0.7397	0.0005	41.13
Error	208	127036.53538084	610.76		STD DEV		ANX Mean
Corrected Total	209	127104.45			24.71		60.09

Source	DF	Anova SS	F Value	PR>F
FL		67.62176202	0.17	0.7397

Dependent Variable : Psychot

Source	DF	Sum of Squares	Mean Square	F Value	PR>F	R. Square	C.V.
Model	1	39.09	39.09	9.19	0.0027	0.04	62.5825
Error	208	804.60	4.25		STD DEV		Psychot Mean
Corrected Total	209	923.65			2.06		3.29

Source	DF	Anova SS	F Value	PR>F
FL		39.09	9.19	0.0027

Table 20 (Contd.)

Dependent Variable : Extra

Source	DF	Sum of Squares	Mean Square	F Value	PR<F	R. Square	C.V.
Model	1	31.04	31.04	1.00	0.1716	0.0089	26.54
Error	208	3437.06	16.49		STD DEV		Extra Mean
Corrected Total	209	3462.10			0 06		15.30

Source	DF	Anova SS	F Value	PR>F
FL	1	31.03	1.98	0.17

Dependent Variable : Neurot

Source	DF	Sum of Squares	Mean Square	F Value	PR<F	R. Square	C.V.
Model		200.33	200.33	10.72	0.0017	0.006	37.66
Error	208	4117.43	19.79		STD DEV		Neurot Mean
Corrected Total	209	4317.76			4.453		11.81

Source	DF	Anova SS	F Value	PR>F
FL	1	200.32716743	10.12	0.0017

FL	N	ANX	Psychot	Extra	Neurot
1	09	59.4849405	2.83038324	15.7070707	12.8484548
2	111	60.6216215	3.70270270	14.9369359	10.8918919

the variables were reversed. That is, variables, that were till now treated as response variables were given the status of classification variables. The notations used in this analysis for independent variables are the following :

Originality (O)

Flexibility (F)

Fluency (FL)

The results of the ANOVA treatments are presented in Tables 18 through 20.

In this case the classification variables are originality, flexibility, and fluency scores. Each of the classification variable has been considered at two levels viz. high and low. The dependent variables are anxiety, neuroticism, psychoticism, and extraversion. Perusal of Tables 18 through 20 yields the following results :

1. The high and low scorers on originality differ significantly on anxiety ; the high scorers scoring high on anxiety, and the low scores scoring low on anxiety.

2. The high and low scorers on originality differ significantly on neuroticism ; the high scorers scoring high on neuroticism, and the low scorers scoring low on neuroticism.

3. The high and low scorers on originality differ significantly on psychoticism ; the high scorers scoring low on psychoticism, and low scorers scoring high on psychoticism.

4. The high and low scorers on originality do not differ on extraversion.

5. The high and the low scorers on flexibility do not differ on anxiety.

6. The high and low scorers on flexibility differ signifi-

cantly on neuroticism, the high scorers scoring high on neuroticism, and the low scorers scoring low on neuroticism.

7. The high and the low scorers on flexibility differ significantly on psychoticism, the high scorers scoring low on psychoticism, and the low scorers scoring high on psychoticism.

8. The high and low scorers on flexibility do not differ on extraversion.

9. The high and low scorers on fluency do not differ on anxiety.

10. The high and low scorers on fluency differ significantly on neuroticism, the high scorers scoring high on neuroticism, and the low scorers scoring low on neuroticism.

11. The high and low scorers on fluency differ significantly on psychoticism, the high scorers scoring low on psychoticism, and the low scorers scoring high on psychoticism.

12. The high and low scorers on fluency do not differ on extraversion.

CHAPTER VI

Findings and Conclusions

One of the basic purposes of a scientific research activity is to relate the observed facts (i e. immediate discovery) to some organization of a system. It amounts to what Arieti (1976) names, individualizing some underlying communality or connection between things that were deemed dissimilar or unrelated before. If, however, some of the observed facts do not seem to fit in a system, such apparent contradictions should be explainable with valid reasons. When the observed facts are related to a system, "the immediate discovery may lead to additional properties hidden in the class or system" (Arieti 1976). It, then, becomes an innovation.

This humble piece of research, does not attain that lofty ideal of innovation. It merely tends to relate some of the observed facts of affective human domain to its creative potentiality. In this chapter an effort has been made to explain various observations in the light of theoretical orientation of creative thinking and anxiety, as well as anxiety-proneness. Secondly, the results are discussed to show how these findings are concurrent with some of the empirical studies already conducted in the field. At places, some of the observations did not concur the findings of some other investigators. In such cases, attempts have been made to fathom plausible reasons for these disagreements.

DISCUSSION OF RESULTS RELATING TO PRIMARY PURPOSES OF THE STUDY

Anxiety and Creative Thinking

Before proceeding to discuss results relating to the two variables—anxiety and creative thinking—it will be worthwhile to repeat the hypotheses concerning them. Hypotheses concerning the relationship between anxiety and creative thinking are mentioned as No. 1 and No. 2 (Chapter IV) which read as under :

Hypotheses No. 1. To evoke sufficiently creative responses to some stimuli a minimal level of anxiety is essential.

Hhpotheses No. 2. There is some optimal level of anxiety which contributes most to evoke creative responses. Further increase in anxiety does not affect creative thinking scores appreciably.

From the analysis of results in regard to relationship between creative thinking abilities and anxiety, it has been observed that individuals at different levels of anxiety do not give identical or similar creative responses. In the case of originality, the scores at low level of anxiety are quite low. But at high and average levels of anxiety the originality scores are significantly higher than at low level. In the light of these resulls it may be safely inferred that to evoke sufficiently original responses some average to high level of anxiety is needed. It further implies that for sufficiently original responses to occur there is a minimal level of anxiety required. This minimal level of anxiety may be called the *threshold* level. The threshold value of anxiety, in the case of the present sample, is found to be 44 on the DPI (44 is the score on the DPI which marks the average anxious from the low anxious in this group). From these results, perhaps, a safe conclusion can also be drawn regarding the optimum level of anxiety needed to evoke original responses. The mean anxiety of the average anxious group i.e. score on the DPI, can serve as the best index for the optimum level in this regard, because, after this level is reached further increase in anxiety does not significantly decrease or increase scores on originality. Hypotheses No. 1 and Hypotheses No. 2 are accepted with originality as one of the creative thinking abilities.

Regarding the effect of anxiety on flexibility and fluency the results indicate a difference when these are compared with those of originality as response variable. The flexibility, and fluency at different levels of anxiety (i.e. high, average and low) do not differ significantly among themselves. On the basis of these results, Hypotheses No. 1 and No. 2, therefore, are only partially accepted. That is, to evoke sufficiently creative responses, it is only in the case of originality as creative thinking ability that some *minimal* as well as some *optimal* level of anxiety is needed. In the case of flexibility and fluency, however, particular level of anxiety does not substantially affect scores on these abilities.

Hypothesis No. 1 was framed considering anxiety as an energizing drive (Spence, 1956) or as general physiological arousal or activation as conceived and reported by Cannon, Yerkes-Dodson (1908), Korchin (1962), Eysenck (1967), Cattell and Scheier (1961). In fact the differential behaviour of anxiety on different creative thinking abilities may be attributed to the logical differences that lie among these abilities.

Secondly, human behaviour is usually determined by a complex constellation within which a number of factors interact to produce behaviour at any given moment. It requires multi-factor approach to conduct experiment so as to reach unequivocal results.

In the case of flexibility and fluency some extraneous factors might be interacting, some of which have been taken in the present study, and their interactions found out. On flexibility the interaction of psychoticism and extraversion with anxiety is clearly visible. The F-ratios in the case of this second order interaction, X*P*E, is 5.5 which is significant at .0044 level of significance. This significant interaction substantiates the logic of the argument made as above. According to this interaction, anxiety alone is not sufficient to determine the creative potentiality in terms of flexibility and fluency. Rather, a conglomerate of a high level of anxiety, high level of extraversion and low level of psychoticism constitutes the optimum condition to evoke creative (flexible) responses. Similarly one could find some such interactions with other variables to evoke fluent responses. The investigator, with his limitation of time and space, could not include many of such extraneous factors. Further research may be undertaken to determine the nature and extent of such interactions. The Hypotheses No. 1 and No. 2, therefore, are modified in the light of the findings and now can be read as under :

Hypotheses No. 1 : To evoke sufficiently 'original' responses to some stimuli a minimal level of anxiety is essential.

Hypotheses No. 2 : There is some optimal level of anxiety which contributes most to evoke 'original' responses. Further increase in anxiety level does not appreciably change originality scores of individuals.

Neuroticism and Creative Thinking

The hypotheses framed to describe the relationship between neuroticism and creative thinking is No. 5 which reads as under :

Hypolheses No. 5 : There is some optimal level of neuroticism which contributes most to evoke creative responses.

When viewed from the point of view of genetic purity of trait between neuroticism and anxiety, it is neuroticism that can be considered relatively in a purer form. It is assumed to be more of a genotype, whereas, anxiety is considered as phenotype. For this reason, therefore, it is some times termed as anxiety-proneness, a fundamental and direct source of anxiety. It is considered as the genetically determined sensitivity to some stimuli. With a view to see how this genetic emotional lability is related to creative thinking abilities, the results were obtained (Tables 12 through 14 ; and 12a through 14a).

The results indicate that neuroticism constitutes a highly significant factor to predict the creative thinking behaviour of individuals. (F-ratio in each case of originality, flexibility and fluency are highly significant). From the results of Duncan's tests applied on these significant Fs, it is obvious that a high level of neuroticism is more favourable to evoke highly creative responses on all the abilities of creative thinking.

Secondly, it is further revealed that the higher the level of neuroticism, the higher will be the scores on component abilities of creative thinking. Moreover, when the two contrast groups on creative thinking abilities (25% upper—the high creatives, and 25% lower – the low creatives) are compared, it is found that the high creative group is significantly higher on neuroticism than the low creative group. These findings are thus consistent with that of Spence (1964), who conceived of anxiety (Anxiety proneness) as an energizing drive.

There is much controversy regarding the effect of anxiety or anxiety-proneness on cognitive processes. Such differences may be attributed to taking different views of anxiety. Those who tend to prove anxiety as an interfering variable with these processes, consider anxiety as a phenotype, where as those who consider anxiety as an energizing force, take it as a genotype.

In fine, the results of the present study are quite consistent with the general arousal or activation theory of anxiety. It is, perhaps, neuroticism (a general proneness to anxiety) of which the great existentialist, Kierkegaard, spoke so high.

Regarding hypothesis No. 5, which was framed under the aegis of activation theory of anxiety, the evidence is clear to accept it fully. Though creative thinking scores at the three levels of neuroticism are in ascending order of neuroticism, yet the difference of means, between level 3 and level 2, is higher than difference of means between level 2 and level 1 in the case of each of the three components of creative thinking.

Status of Anxiety and Neuroticism in the Context of Creative Thinking Abilities

The results discussed just before impel one to consider the relative status of anxiety and neuroticism to trace some etiological or other such relationships between the two. When the status of anxiety and neuroticism in this respect are compared, the results indicate some differences. At lower levels, the two, anxiety and neuroticism, behave similarly on creative thinking tasks. But after the average level is reached they seem to take different paths with regard to their effects on creative thinking. This happens particularly in the case of flexibility and fluency as response variables. The flexibility and fluency scores at different levels of anxiety cannot be differentiated significantly from one another. In the case of originality, however, the impact of neuroticism and anxiety is very similar, except that with the increase in neuroticism originality scores go on increasing, but rate of increase decreases. This differential effect of the two variables can probably be explained taking into considerations the hypothesized nature of the two variables. Both these variables act as drive. But anxiety, being phenotype, develops perhaps as a result of interaction of the frustrating conditions present in the environment. Such conditions of the environment may also affect the ego strength adversely. The ego-strength, though not a factor in the present study, is commonly accepted as a significant factor to evoke creative responses.

On the basis of these results one may hold that whereas anxiety provides a challenge, and acts as a drive and as a motivating force to counteract the obstacles, it may also tend to disrupt the normal Ego functioning under certain conditions of the environment and the person. Berkeley Studies also show that a creative person may be higher on psycho-pathological aspects of MMPI, yet he always has a strong Ego. This theoretical account tending to explain the behaviour of anxiety in comparison to neuroticism needs further empirical verification with ego-strength as one of the variables.

The results relating to neuroticism and creativity can, perhaps, be interpreted more easily. It is clear from the results that neuroticism constitutes a significant factor to predict creative thinking behaviour of individuals. In this case the originality, flexibility or fluency scores are not adversely affected even at higher levels of it. The reason for the same may be that neuroticism is only genetically determined sensitivity, and is expressed in terms of emotionality of behaviour. Therefore, neuroticism, even at higher levels, instead of acting as a disrupting force to creative thinking, increases sensitivity of observation, heightens his critical faculties and, thus, enables one to try various ways to solve a problem.

Nature of Relationship between Anxiety, Neuroticism, and Creative Thinking

To test the nature of the said relationship hypotheses No. 3 and 4 were framed. These hypotheses, for the sake of convenience and clarity of discussion, are repeated as under :

Hypotheses No. 3 : The relationship between anxiety and creative thinking ability is curvilinear.

Hypotheses No. 4 : The relationship between neuroticism and creative thinking ability is curvilinear.

The rationale of these hypotheses was that human personality is simultaneously and variously affected by many forces, intrinsic as well as extrinsic. Whenever one tries to find the relationship, say, between anxiety and originality, it cannot be measured in its pure form. It is like projectiles in physics that whenever some object is thrown upward at an angle less than

90 degree the path described by it cannot be a straight line, because the force of gravitation is acting upon it at all times and points in space. So, there is more likelihood that the relationship between anxiety (or anxiety-proneness) and creative thinking abilities be better described through some curves instead of straight lines. F-ratios of simple straight line regressions, taking two variables at a time, were computed which are presented in table 15 through 17.

The highly significant 'Fs' in these cases clearly prove that the regression is not straight line. And whenever regression is not straight line it can only be described through a curve of some type. McNemar (1969, pp. 311-317) states that if the 'F' ratios of regression are high enough, test of linearity stands rejected ; and the relationship should be better described through a curve.

To have a still better insight into the nature of these relationships, regression curves were drawn. From these curves it was obvious that in the case of neuroticism as classification variable the curvature is not inverted U type ; that it does not follow Yerkes-Dodson Law. The mean creative thinking socres at the three levels of neuroticism also tell the same story. In the case of anxiety, on the other hand, the curves suggest that the relationship tends to follow Yerkes-Dodson Law. It is further substantiated by the fact that the means at average level of anxiety are highest, whereas at low and high levels, the means show decrement.

To interpret results concerning neuroticism and creativity one can refer them to Spence's (1964) concept of anxiety, who considers anxiety as a general energizing drive. The results further are in consonance with general activation theory—the theory of general physiological arousal first proposed by Cannon (Levitt, 1968). Spence views anxiety as a force that motivates an individual to perform. His theory does not extend to a level of drive which disrupts performance. In the present study, the same is found true of neuroticism.

High and Low Creatives on Personality Variables

It was thought desirable to see whether the high and the low creatives on each of the component abilities of creative thinking differ in regard to their scores on anxiety, neuroticism, psychoticism, and extraversion. Though the analysis is interesting in itself, yet it is related to hypotheses No. 1 to No. 5 of the study.

It is clear from the result mentioned in Chapter V that the high creatives on originality, flexibility, and fluency are significantly higher on neuroticism. This finding gives added support to hypotheses No. 5, and also to Spence's theory of anxiety (proneness) as an energizing force.

When the high and the low creatives were compared on anxiety as dependent variable, the high creatives on originality were significantly high on anxiety (significant at .05 level of significance). This finding is consistent with the earlier finding i.e., when originality was tested at different levels of anxiety. The high and the low creatives in flexibility and fluency, however, were not found to differ significantly.

The observed fact that anxiety is not highly related to creative thinking as neuroticism is, may be explained slightly differently also. Development of anxiety as a trait is not solely dependent upon its genotypical cause i.e., neuroticism. Rather, certain other genetic factors, in addition to neuroticism together with the conditions present in the environment do cause anxiety. For example, psychoticism as a trait of human personality, if present in substantial degrees, may also become a cause for the development of anxiety or vice versa. This fact that increased level of psychoticism adds to the anxiety level is discussed above in this chapter. Secondly, an interaction of high psychoticism level always tends to limit creative responses. Further, it is also established through this study as well as through many others that psychoticism is positively related to behavioural rigidity, which limits creative self-expression.

It implies that not all kinds of anxious persons tend to be creative. To find out how and with what kinds of persons anxiety facilitates creative self-expression, further research is needed.

Extraversion and Creative Thinking

With extraversion as one of the response variables hypotheses No. 6 was framed which reads as under :

Hypotheses No. 6 : Extraverts are more creative than introverts.

Kinard White (1975), as quoted earlier (Chapter III), found that extraverts give more original responses to some stimuli. To test White's findings on Indian population the design was made. But the result of the present investigation clearly prove that with originality as response variables there is no significant difference between extraverts and introverts (high and low on extraversion). The F-ratios of the analyses of variance (Tables 9 through 11 and also Tables 9c through 11c) clearly supports this conclusion. Kinard Whites's finding, therefore, is not supported by these findings. White had stated extraverts to be more original than introverts.

In regard to flexibility and fluency of extraverts the results support hypotheses No. 6. It is concluded that extraverts are more creative then introverts except in the case of originality as creative ability. Hypotheses No. 6 therefore is only partially accepted and is re-written in modified form as : "Extraverts are more flexible and fluent in giving responses to some stimuli than introverts. However, extraverts and introverts do not differ on originality." Regarding the effect of this dimension of personality some very interesting results are in view. Extraversion enters into significant interactions with some other variables to evoke creative responses.

With anxiety as the main classifying variable the significant interaction that extraversion enters into is X*P*E, which is significant in the cases of originality, and flexibility. This interaction appears to be the most important *response-surface* of creative thinking.

Similarly, the results of Tables 12 through 14, i.e., where neuroticism is substituted for anxiety, indicate the following significant interactions in which extraversion enters :

(i) Y*E with all the three, originality, flexibility, and fluency as dependent variables.

(ii) Y*P*E with only flexibility as dependent variables.

What is further revealed from the results of these interactions is that whenever extraversion interacts with anxiety or neuroticism, it is always the high extravert who gives more creative responses.

In fine, it can be said that nature of original responses may not be affected by one's position merely on E-I (Extraversion-Introversion) continuum ; but when low psychoticism and high anxiety/neuroticism are simultaneously found to be present in the high extravert, the creative (original) response may be frequent.

The fact that flexibility and fluency of responses depend upon one's position on this continuum of E-I, may be explained in terms of cortical 'inhibition-excitation' theory of Eysenck (Eysenck, 1967). Under this theory an extravert shows maximal cortical inhibition and, hence, he is behaviourally most uninhibited. Further, it is quite reasonable to maintain that for more fluent and flexible responses uninhibited behaviour is needed. The uninhibited attitude under conditions of high motivation works all the more better for evoking such responses. The motivating factor is provided by the anxiety/neuroticism level of an individual. Again, because an extravert tends to interact more fully with things outside, he is, therefore, capable of using more categories in giving responses ; and hence, he can give a large number of responses also than his counterpart. Di-Scipio (1971) also gave similar results in this regard.

Hysterics and Dysthemics on Creative Thinking

Hypothesis No. 7 in this regard was constructed which states that hysterics (persons high on both neuroticism and extraversion) are more creative than dysthemics (persons high on neureticism but low on extraversion). The rationale for this hypothesis was derived from Eysenck's theory of personality (Eysenck 1960, 1967). Eysenck hypothesized that introverted neurotics (dysthemics) were rigid but extraverted neurotics (hysterics) were not. Secondly, Pervin (1960) investigated into the relationship between neuroticism and rigidity (as opposed to flexibility of responses). His findings were that different kinds of neurotics differ in regart to the extent of rigidity on various kinds of tasks.

The results of the present investigation confirm Hypothesis No. 7 and, thus, are consistent with Eysenck's conceptual framework of extraversion and neuroticism. The results can be seen from Tables, 12, 13 and 14 (Chapter V), wherein, each case 'Fs' are significant at .001 level of significance. The tables of LS Means showed that mean originality, flexibility and fluency scores of hysterics are significantly higher than that of dysthemics. Watson (1971) also proved that introverted neurotics are rigid. Seemingly, the results may contradict the findings of Berkeley Studies (Mackinon, 1966, p. 154) which state that creative person, in general, tend towards introversion (in Jungian Typology). The introverts of Jung are very much akin to introverted-neurotics of Eysenck. But the contradiction may not be real. In Berkeley studies, the creative groups taken were "known groups of creatives" whereas in the present study, the experiment was conducted on potentially creatives, who need social recognition, and are yet to actualize themselves. Nevertheless, it is strongly recommended that more studies be done by taking groups of potentially creatives, as well as of "known groups" of creatives. The personality patterns of these groups should be more thoroughly studied on Indian population with a view to point to personality differences, if any, between these two types of creatives.

Sex Differences in Creative Thinking

With a view to study the sex differences in creative thinking hypotheses No. 9, 10 and 11 were framed which read as under :

Hypotheses No. 9 : In general, males and females do not differ in regard to their creative thinking abilities.

Hypotheses No. 10 : At average to high level of anxiety males are more creative than females.

Hypotheses No. 11 : At average to high level of neuroticism males are more creative than females.

The results of the analysis of variance (Tables 9 through 11) pertaining to main effects show that males and females do not differ in their capacities to creative thinking. Hypothesis No. 9, which states that males and females do not differ in regard to their creative thinking abilities, therefore, holds good. But when the sex differences on creative thinking abilities are viewed in relation to anxiety/neuroticism, one can observe some interesting results. Looking into this interaction Y* Sex, it is observed that F-ratios of this interaction are significant in the case of originality, and flexibility as dependent variables. The table of LS means and SEMs in these cases further revealed that at average level of neuroticism males are significantly higher on each of the creative thinking abilities except on fluency. It implies that under conditions of sufficient motivation or stress males can give more original and flexible responses than females. In the case of fluency, however, the interaction Y* Sex is not found significant at all.

Psychoticism and Creative Thinking

Psychoticism, as explained earlier in Chapter IV, is a newly emerging concept as a dimension of personality, which is present in varying degrees in all individuals. More simply it connotes 'toughmindedness-tendermindedness' dimension.

Results relating to psychoticism and creative thinking abilities, presented in Tables 9 through 11, clearly indicate a negative relationship between them. The high 'P' scorers are significantly lower on all creative thinking abilities and low 'P' scorers high. When the high and low creative were compared, the high creatives were found to be significantly low on psychoticism ; while low creatives were significantly high on psychoticism. Hypotheses No. 8 which reads thal "Individuals high on psychoticism are less creative than those low on psychoticism," therefore, is fully accepted.

To explain the results one can circumvent a bit by involving behavioural rigidity—an established trait of high 'P' scorers (Watson, 1967). From Watson's study it is clear that a high 'P' scorer would be more rigid and less fluent verbally. He may, however, sometimes give responses that seem to be remote and strange but such responses of a high 'P' scorer (especially of a schizophrenic) are far from being called original (Arieti, 1976), Such thoughts are indeed bizarre. Because of being overloaded with mere primary process congnitions, they are deprived of verbal flexibility and other secondary process cognitions ; hence, cannot be termed truly creative.

Discussion of Results Relating to Secondary Purposes of the Study

After discussing the results in regard to hypotheses relating to primary purposes of the study, it is thought necessary to reflect a bit on other results, viz., those relating to secondary purposes also. The necessity and importance of these results will be clear from the discussion that follows.

Distribution of Anxiety, Psychoticism, Extraversion and Neuroticism in the Population

Regarding distribution of anxiety, psychoticism, extraversion and neuroticism in the poulation, Hypotheses No. 10 was framed. This hypothesis reads that 'anxiety, neuroticism, extraversion, and psychoticism are all normally distributed traits.' Data collected on those variables are discussed below.

Referring to univariate statistics presented in Table 4, it is observed that anxiety, extraversion, and neuroticism are almost normally distributed traits. Psychoticism, however, is found to be highly skewed (Skewness 9.56, N=762). Apparently this finding is not consistent with what Eysenck (1975) posited. According to him psychoticism, extraversion, and neuroticism are normally distributed traits of haman personality. Indeed the contradiction is only apparent. Eysenck and Eysenck (1976, pp. 70-71) themselves found such deviations. According to the authors, several of the distributions deviate markedly from normality, being positively or negatively skewed. The authors further observed that "the observed distribution of (P) scores depends upon such factors as choice of items, the percentage of endorsement of particular items chosen... Ideally, of course, one would select items in such a way that normality of distribution could be obtained, but this is less important than other criteria we have had in mind for the selection of items, and consequently we have not used scores distribution in considering items for conclusion'' (Parenthesis added). On psychoticism dimension of personality the authors reported mean 'P'=2.7 and $\sigma=2.3$ in the case of female group, while the mean=4 and $\sigma=3.2$ in the case of male group.

The findings of the investigator are quite consistent with those of the authors of 'P' scale. Mean P and of P is to be given here for direct comparison. In the light of the findings and discussion, it is reasonable to hold that anxiety, extraversion, and neuroticism are normally distributed. The normality of distribution of psychoticism is highly doubtful, since, in the present sample, the skewness is highly significant and very high. Hypothesis No. 10 is partially accepted which can now be read as : Of the three dimensions of personality extraversion and neuroticism are normally distributed traits ; psychoticism, however, is positively skewed.'

Orthogonality of RelatioLship Between the Three Dimensions of Personality

While constructing EPQ, Eysenck and Eysenck (1975) claimed that the three dimensions of Personality, viz., Extraversion, Neuroticism, and Psychoticism are independent of each other and, hence, orthogonal. Keeping in view the aforesaid position regarding mutual relationship between the three dimensions of personality, hypothesis No. 14 was framed which reads : "There is orthogonality of relationship between Neuroticism, Extraversion, and Psychoticism."

The findings of this research (Tables 6 through 8) indicate that neuroticism and extraversion, and neuroticism and psychoticism have negligible relationships. But the Pearson 'r' between Psychoticism and extraversion ($r=0.32$) is significant statistically. It implies that these two variables are not mutually exclusive. The posited orthogonality of 'P' and 'E', thus, is highly doubtful. Therefore, hypothesis No. 14 of this study is only partially accepted at present. It is therefore recommended that the relationship between P and E should further be verified on different samples.

Relationship between Neuroticism and Anxiety

The correlation matrices (Tables 5 through 8a) indicate, in this regard, that Pearson 'rs' between anxiety and neuroticism are positive and highly significant statistically. The observed 'rs' in the male sample, in the female sample, and in the total sample are .77, .57 and .66 respectively. Hypothesis No. 15 which states that "there is a positive and high relationship between anxiety and neuroticism," is, therefore, accepted fully. The said hypothesis was made under the assumption that the two, anxiety and neuroticism, are conceptually dependent upon each other. Neuroticism is supposed to be genetically determined sensitivity whose manifestation after interaction with environmental conditions is anxiety. Moreover, Eysenck called neuroticism anxiety-proneness (Fischer 1970, p. 74).

Psychoticism and Anxiety

Hypothesis No. 13 states that psychoticism and anxiety are positively related. The hypothesis in question is based upon the assumption that high 'P' scorers are by nature solitary, apathetic, inhumane, rigid and self-seekers. Such traits come in conflict with the general interest of the social group. They tend to seek recognition and satisfaction through ways that often are frightening to others. Their social behaviours are not liked by others, instead, positively condemned and checked. Consequently, they get frustrated or become hostile, and eventually a vicious circle starts. This considerably adds to their general anxiety.

The results of the present study (Tables 5 through 8) show high positive relationship ($r=.37$, $N=762$) between psychoticism and anxiety. It implies that persons high on psychoticism are also usually high on anxiety. Therefore, Hypotheses No. 13 is fully accepted.

In the light of the findings arrived at and as presented in Chapter V and VI of this work, the investigator feels satisfied (though only partially) regarding various relationships that were theoretically conceived and empirically verified. To a greater extent, he found a concordance between such theoretical conceptualization and empirical observation, though at places he found a gap. In such a case the investigator tried to explain the variance to the best of his abilities and understanding. But the world is very large and complex ; and the causes of phenomena that occur in it are varied and many. To analyse human behaviour (which is so diversely affected by many forces simultaneously), with a view to predict it for certain, is simply not possible for him. What for certain he can claim is an honest effort to seek, to know and to discover ; but what he has sought, known, or discovered is not a universal truth. In this vast flow of time and space the investigator's view is merely a speck which may have some utility at this point of time and space. The investigator submits that this humble piece of research is primarily conceptual in nature. The investigator was mainly occupied with the question, "What goes on in the consciousness of a creative student, vis-a-vis a non-creative one ?"

Educational Implications of the Main Findings

One of the important findings of the present study is that highly original students have significantly higher scores on anxiety as well as on neuroticism than the less creative (original) ones. But such an observation should not lead one to suppose that anxiety is the cause of originality. Reflections on the nature of the creative process, product, and person have already made it obvious that a creative (original) individual is in the minority of one, and there are few persons who can tolerate being a minority of one (Torrance, 1969). Again, attitudinally, a creative child is non-conforming. Such factors cause psychological estrangement, which sometimes result in raising general anxiety level. Viewed in this way, first an individual is creative (original), he then gets alienated from the social group, and thus feels anxious.

But originality (creative thinking) may also be traced to have some causal connection with anxiety/neuroticism. If the individual confronts some situation that tends to disturb the 'homeostasis' of one's ego with the environment, the individual feels anxious, or the neuroticism level is increased. In this way anxiety may cause a physiological arousal, and may act as a drive, a motivating or energizing force. The findings have proved that such an arousal is facilitating upto a certain optimal level of anxiety/neuroticism. But if anxiety crosses the optimal level it tends to limit original responses. Both of these explanations of the concomitance of anxiety/neuroticism and original thinking have significant educational implications. Not recognizing or consciously neglecting creative children on the basis of their uncommon behaviour makes them highly anxious. This heightened anxiety in certain cases may help manifestation of their psychoticism level ; and consequently, such children adopt an aggressive and hostile attitude. The study has proved that high level of psychoticism always limits creative responses. Such children become insensitive to problems of true creative nature. Their ability to sense gaps in knowledge is marred. In order to avoid such a situation following suggestions are offered :

1. The uncommon discoveries of creative individual should not meet social disapproval, for, with that disapproval the child will suffer anguish. Consequently, either the child will repress his creativity and become most obedient, and, hence, conforming, or he may become aggressive and hostile.

2. Some of the ideas of creative children are often what Torrance (1969) calls, 'silly' or 'wild'. The teachers and parents must recognize this truth, and should not get annoyed on manifestation of such a behaviour. Instead, they should help children relate such ideas to socially and logically desired ways of thinking.

3. Sometimes the adults are not able to evaluate the unusual ideas. Such a behaviours on the part of teachers become a cause of aggression or extreme anxiety. The situation comes more quickly if such unusual ideas are rejected by the teachers. Some of the children, on receiving such a treatment, raise their general psychoticism level, and if the treatment is prolonged the student may turn sociopath ; else, he may get overwhelmed by anxiety and turn neurotic.

4. Some of the original or creative children are often not well rounded. Such children should not be discouraged and condemned for their failures in fields other than the field of their special interest. General encouragement and appreciation for the special ability of such children is likely to have an all round good impact on their performance.

5. Anxiety has some positive aspects also. If anxiety is developed as a general trait, it increases the general sensitivity of children to sense gaps in knowledge. The findings of the present investigation indeed are

associated with such anxiety/neuroticism. Anxiety in the form of a general trait enables children to give original responses. The study has proved that to evoke sufficiently original responses a threshold level of anxiety is needed. Children, therefore, should be provided with challenging situations. Such challenging situations coupled with encouraging behaviour of the teacher will go a long way in stimulating the child for creative solutions to problems. Challenging situations, for a short while, may check the tensional discharge and consequently, some level of anxiety may be produced, but ensuing of such instances of anxiety are likely to impel children seek new path ways, leading to creative self expression.

6. The other finding that hysterics are more creative than dysthemics leads one to understand that our attitude towards introvert students should be such as to reduce their anxiety level. The study has shown that increased level of anxiety is debilitating for introverts, while extraverts work better under moderate to high level of anxiety. Educationally such finding, therefore, is immensely useful to treat differentially these two categories of children. In the case of extraverts the situational contingencies may be so arranged that they lead to increase in anxiety, whereas, in the case of introverts, these should be so organised that students get constant encouragement, thereby reducing the anxiety level, or it is not allowed to develop.

7. We should not brand a particular sex as more creative than the other. Both males and females can be equally creative if a suitable climate is provided to them.

In the end, it can safely be held that to gear up the process of education, especially in the direction of stimulating creativity, the present piece of research seems to be of some value. We, as teachers or psychologists, must study a child's personality vis-a-vis such dimensions, and only that should guide our behaviour and method to make children realize their creative potentialities.

To release the creative potential of youngsters shall be a conscious human help to the natural process of evolution.

Bibliography

Anderson, H.H. (ed.) *Creativity and its Cultivation.* New York : Harper and Row, 1959.

Arieti, S., *The Intrapsychic Self.* New York : Basic Books, 1967.

———————, *Creativity—the Magic Synthesis.* New York : Basic Books, 1976.

Arlow, J.A., and Brenner, C. *Psychological Concepts and Structural Theory,* New York : International Uni. Press, 1964.

Arora, G.L., "A Study of Relationship between anxiety and creative Thinking." *Indian Education Review* (1967) : 91-96.

Averill, J.R. Emotion and Anxiety—Determinants. In Zukerman, M., and Spielberger, C.D. (Eds.), *Emotions and Anxiety.* New Jersey : Lawrence, Erlbaum Associates, 1976.

Barbe, W.B., and Renzulli, J.S, (Eds.) *Psychology and Education of the Gifted.* New York : John Wiley and Sons, 1975.

Barron, F. Needs for Order and Disorder as Motives in Creative Activity. In Gowan et. al. *Creativity and its Educational Implications.* New York : John Wiley and Sons, 1967.

Barron, F., and Welsh, G.S. Artistic Perception as a Possible Factor in Personality Style. *Journal of Psychology*, XXXIII (1952).

Barron, F, Complexity—Simplicity as a Personality Dimension. *Journal of Abnormal and Social Psychology*, 48 (1953) : 163-172.

———— –, The Disposition Towards Originality. In C.W. Taylor (ed.), University of Utah Research Conference on "Identification of Creative Scientific Talent," Utah : Salt Lake City, 1955.

——————, "Originality in Relation to Personality and Intellect," *Journal of Personality* 25 (1957) : 730-742.

Barron, F. "The Psychology, of Imagination". *Scientific American*, 199 : 3 1958 150-170.

————————, *Creativity and Psychological Health : Origins of Personality and Creative Freedom.* Princeton, N.J. : Van Nostrand, 1963.

————————, *Creative and Creative Process*, New York : Holt, Rinehart and Winston, 1969.

Bartlett, F.C., "Types of Imagination." in Stein and Heinz (Annotated Bibliography) *Creativity and Individual*, Glancoe : The Free Press, 1960.

Binswanger, Ludwig , *Being-in-the-World.* Trans. Needleman, Jacob. Harper Torch Books, 1967.

Bowers, P.G , "Effects of Hyponosis and Suggestions of Reduced Defensiveness on Creativity Test Performance." *Journal of Personality*, 35, 11-322.

Brand, Harry., "Kafka's Creative Crisis." *Journal of American Academy of Psychoanalysts*, 1976 : 4(2), 249-260.

Bronowski, J. "The Creative Process." *Scientific American*, 1958 : 3, 150-170.

Bruner, J.S., *On Knowing.* Cambridge, Mass. : Belknap Press, 1962.

Bruner, J.S., *The Process of Education* Cambridge, Mass :, Harvard University Press, 1960.

Buch, M.B. (ed.), *A Survey of Research in Education.* Baroda : CASE, M.S. University of Baroda, 1974.

Buch, M.B., (ed.), *Survey of Research in Education.* Baroda, SERD, 1979.

Buhl, H.R., *Creative Engineering Design.* IOWA : State University Press, 1960.

Cattell, R.B., and Drevdahl, J.E., "A Comparison of Personality Profile (16 PF) of Eminent Researchers with that of Eminent Teachers and Administrators and of the General Population." *B. Journal of Psychology,* 1955 : XLVI 248-61.

Cattell, R.B , and Scheier, I.H., "Nature of Anxiety : A Review of Thirteen Multivariate Analysis." In E.E. Levitt, *The Psychology of Anxiety.* Staples, 1967, 219-230.

Cattell, R.B , and Butcher, H.J., *The Prediction of Achievement and Creativity.* Indiana Polis : Bobbs-Merril, 1968.

Chaudhary, Haridas. *Integral Yoga : The Concept of Harmonius and Creative Living.* London : George Allen and Unwin, 1975.

Dauw, D.C., "Aspirations and Dreams of Creatively Gifted High School Seniors and Comparable Unselected Groups." *Gifted Child Quarterly,* 9 (1965) : 177-182.

Dayton, C. Mitchell, *The Design of Educational Experiment,* New York : McGraw-Hill, 1970.

Dollard, J., and Miller, N., *Personality and Psychotherapy.* New York : McGraw Hill, 1950.

Domino, George, "Primary Process Thinking in Dreams," *Journal of Consulting and Clinical Psychology*, 1976 : 44 (6), 929-932.

Drwal, R.L., "Influence of Emotional Process on Efficiency of Creative Thinking". *Psychological Abstracts*, July to December 1975 : 8902.

Discipio, W.J., Study quoted in H.J. Eysenck, *Measurement of Personality*, Baltimore : University Park Press 1961.

Drevdahl, J.E., "Factors of Importance for Creativity." *Journal of Clinical Psychology*, 12, (1956) : 12-6.

Dutt, N.K., *Psychological Foundations of Education*. Delhi : Doaba House, 1974.

Dutt, N.K. and Gurbaksh Lal, *The Creative Potential and Education*. Ambala : Indian Book Agency, 1977.

Dutt, N.K , *Manual for Dutt Personality Inventory*, Varanasi : Rupa Psychological Centre, 1975.

Dutt, N.K. and Dagaur, B.S., "Creativity and the Child." In *School Education* (Punjab), vol. VI (1), 1980.

Eichbaum, Lange., (1932), in S. Arieti, *Creativity—the Magic Synthesis*. New York : Basic Books Inc , 1976.

Eidelberg, L., (ed.), *Encyclopaedia of Psychoanalysis*. London : Collier—Macmillan, 1968.

Eysenck, H.J., *Experiments in Personality*. London : Routledge and Kegan Paul, 1960.

Eysenck, H J. and Eysenck, S B G., *Psychoticism—as a Dimension of Personality*. London : Hodder and Stonghton, 1976.

Eysenck, H.J., *The Measurement of Personality*. Baltimore : University Park Press, 1976.

Eysenck, H.J. (ed.), *Readings in Extraversion—Introversion : Bearings on Basic Psychological Processes.* London : Staples Press, 1971.

Eysenck, H.J., *The Structure of Human Personality.* London : Methuen and Co. Ltd., 1970.

Fastingbaur, T.R., "Relation of Dogmatism to Creativity (Origence and Intellectance)." *Psychological Reports,* 41 (1977).

Fenichel, O., *The Psychoanalytic Study of Neurosis.* New York : W.W. Norton, 1945 : 703.

Finch, Jeannette M., *Journal Creative Behaviour,* 1977 : 11(3), p. 211.

Fischer, W.F., *Theories of Anxiety,* New York, London: Harper and Row, 1970.

Flanagan, J.C., Definitions and Measurements of Ingenuity. In C.W. Taylor (ed.), The Second (1957), University of Utah Research Conference on the Identification of Creative Scientific Talent, Salt Lake City : University of Utah Press, 1958 : 109-118.

Freud, S., *Character and Anal Eroticism.* Collected Papers New York : Basic Books, vol. 2, 1959.

Freud, S., Types of Onset of Neurosis, (quoted text written 1912), In the Standard edition of Complete Works of S. Freud (Trans. by James Starchey), London : Hogarth, 1958, vol. XII, 231-238, (New York : Basic Books).

Freud, S. 1959), *Inhibitions, Symptoms and Anxiety* (quoted text written in 1927) Trans. by James Strachey, London : Hagarth, 1959, vol. XX.

Freud, S. (1908), "The Relation of Poet to day-dreaming." In Collected Papers, London : Hogarth, 1924 vol. II.

Fromm, Erich, "Escape from Freedom." In Rollo May, *The Meaning of Anxiety*, 1950 : The Ronald Press, 169-176.

Fromm, Erich., "The Creative Attitude". In *Creativity and its Cultivation.* Edited by H.H Anderson, New York : Harper and Row, 1969.

Fromm, Erich., *Escape from Freedom.* New York : Rinehart and Company, Inc., 1941.

Gakhar, S. and Luthra, S., 1973, "Effect of Anxiety Administration on Creative Performance." *Creativity News Letter*, 3, (1974) : 9-17.

Garrett, H.E. *Statistics in Education and Psychology.* Bombay Pfeffer and Simons Ltd., 1966.

Getzels, J.W., and Jackson, P.W., "The Meaning of Giftedness". In Barbe and Renzulli, *Psychology and Education of the Gifted.* New York : John Wiley and Sons, 1975.

Getzels, J.W. and Jackson, P.W., Study of Giftedness—A Multidimensional Approach, in W.B. Barbe and J S. Renzulli (eds.) *Psychology and Education of the Gifted.* New York : John Wiley and Sons, 1975 : 109.

Getzels, J.W. and Jackson, P.W., *Creativity and Intelligence.* Explorations with Gifted Students. New York : Wiley, 1962.

Ghiselin, B., *The Creative Process.* Berkeley : University of California, 1952.

Ghiselin, B., "The Creative Process." In Gowan, Demos and Torrance, (eds.), *Creativity—its Educational Implication*, New York : John Wiley and Sons, 1967.

Greenacre, P., "The Childhood of the Artist" *Psychoanalytic, Study of the Child*, 12 (1957) 47-72, New York : International Universities, 1957.

Goldstein, K , *Human Natures in the light of Psychopathology.* New York : Schocken, 1963.

————, *The Organism : A Holistic Approach to Biology derived from Pathological Data in Man.* Boston : Beacon, 1963.

Gordon, W.J., *Synectics : The Development of Creative Capacity*, New York : Harper and Row, 1963.

Gough, H.G , *California Psychological Inventory Manual.* California Consulting Psychologist Press, 1957.

Goyal, R.P., "A Study of Some Personality Correlates of Creativity in Secondary School Teachers under Training." Panjab University Doctoral Dissertation, 1973.

Guilford, J.P., "Psychometric Approach to Creativity." In Gowan, Demos and Torrance (eds.), *Creativity, its Educational Implication.* John Wiley and Sons, 1967.

————, and Merrified, P.R., *The Structure of Intellect Model : Its Uses and Implications.* Los Angeles : University of Southern California Press, 1960.

————, "Creative Ability in Arts," Psychological Review, LXIV, 1957 : 110-18.

————, "Creativity." *American Psychologist*, V (1959) : 444-54.

Guiford, J.P., "Traits of Creativity and Its Cultivation." In H.H. Anderson (ed.), *Creativity and Its Cultivation.* New York : Harper, 1959, 142-61.

————, "Three faces of Intellect." In W.B. Barbe and J.S. Renzulli, *Psychology and Education of the Guifled.* New York : Irvington Publisher, Inc., 1975.

Gowan, J.C., Demos, G.D., and Torrance, E.P., *Creativity : Its Educational Implication.* John Wiley and Sons, 1967.

Hallman, R J., (1963), Necessary and Sufficient Conditions. In Gowan, Demos and Torrance, *Creativity—Its Educational Implications.* John Wiley and Sons., 1967, 19.

Hammer, Emanuel F. "Artistic Creativity, Giftedness or Sickness." *Arts Psychotherapy,* 1975 : 2(2), 173-175.

Horney, Karen. *Our Inner Conflicts : A Constructive Theory of Neurosis.* New York : W.W. Norton and Co., Inc., 1945.

Hassan, Qamar., and Khan, Sham Shur, R., "Creativity, Intelligence and Temperament." *Psychologia,* 1976, vol. 19(4), 193-199.

Hutchinson, E.D., *How to Think Creatively.* New York : Abingdon, Cokesbury, 1949.

Jackobson, A.C., Genius : Some Reevaluations. In., S. Arieti, *Creativity—the Magic Synthesis.* New York : Basic Books Inc., 1976, 356.

Jacobson, Edith., "The Affects and Their Pleasure—Unpleasure Qualities in Relation to the Psychic discharge Process." In M. Rudolph, Lownstein (ed.), *Drives, Affects and Behaviour.* New York : International Universities Press, 1953.

Jacobson, Edith., *Psychotic Conflict and Reality.* The Hogarth Peess, 1967.

Jha, S.K., *An Analysis of Certain Dimensions of Creativity.* Bombay : Himalaya Publishing House, 1978.

Jung, C.G., *Psychological Types.* New York : Harcourt, Brace, 1946.

————, "The Archetypes and the Collective Unconscious." *Collected Works.* New York : Pantheon, 1959.

Kandil, Shaker A., "Torrance, E.P., Further Verification of High Creative Potential Among Emotionally Disturbed and Behaviour Disordered Children." *Journal of Creative Behaviour*, vol. 12(4), Creative Education Foundation, 1978.

Kierkegaard, S., *The Concept of Dread.* (Original text written in 1844, Trans. with Introduction by Walter Lowrie) Priceton, University Press, 1944.

Koestler, A., *The Act of Creation.* New York : Macmillon, 1964.

————————, *Insight and Outlook.* New York : Macmillon, 1949.

Korchin, S.J., Anxiety and Cognition. In E.E. Levitt, *The Psychology of Anxiety.* Staples, 1967 : p. 230.

Kogan, Nathan. "Creativity and Sex Differences." *Journal of Creative Behaviour*, 1974 : 8(1), 1-14.

Kris, L., "On Preconscious Mental Processes." *Psychoanalytic Quarterly*, 19, 542, Reprinted in Kris, 1952.

————————, *Psychoanalytic Explorations in Art.* New York : International Universities Press, 1952.

————————, "Psychoanalysis and Study of Imagination." In Sten and Heinz, *Creativity and Individual.* Glenco : The Free Press, 1960 : (Annotated Bibliography), 1953.

Kubie, L.S., *Neurotic Distortion of the Creative Process.* Lawrence, Kansas : University of Kansas Press, 1958.

Levitt, E.E., *The Psychology of Anxiety.* London : Stapple Press, 1968, p. 144.

Lombroso, C., The Man of Genius. In S. Arieti, *Creativity—The Magic Synthesis.* New York : Basic Books Inc., 1976.

Lowenfeld, V., "The Nature of Creative Activity," an Annotated Bibliography, in Stein and Heinz, *Creativity and the Individual.* Glencoe : The Free Press, 1960.

McAllister, J., "Fould's Continuum of Personal Illness and the 16 P F.". In *British Journal of Psychiatry*, 117, 106-110.

MacKinnon, D.W., "Personality Correlates of Creativity." In Gown, Demos and Torrance *Creativity—Its Educational Implications.* John Wiley and Sons, 1967.

————————, (1962) "Nature and Nurture of Creative Talent." In Barbe and Renzulli, *Psychology and Education of the Gifted.* Irvington, Publishing Inc., 1975.

MacKinnon, D.W., "What Makes a Person Creative," in, *Theory Into Practice*, V (No. 4, 1966), p. 154.

McRenolds, Paul, "Assimilation and Anxiety," in C. Zukerman, and Spielberger, *Emotions and Anxiety.* Lowrence Erlbaum Associates, 1976.

Martindale, Colin, "Creativity, Consciousness and Arousal." *Journal of Altered States of Consciousness*, 1977 : 3(1), pp. 69-87.

Maslow, A.H., *Towards a Psychology of Being*, NJD : van. Nostrand, 1962.

————————, "Defence and Growth," in W.B. Barbe and J.S. Renzulli, *Psychology and Education of the Gifted.* John Wiley and Sons, 1975, p. 109.

————————, "Creativity in Self-Actualizing People," in H.H. Anderson (ed.), *Creativity Its Cultivation.* New York : Harper, 1959.

May, Rollo., *The Meaning of Anxiety*, New York : The Ronald Press Company, 1950.

May, R. "The Nature of Creativity", in H.H. Anderson (ed.), *Creativity and its Cultivation.* New York : Harper, 1959 ; 65-68,

McGuire, C., "Dimensions of Creativity," in (Annotaled Bibliography), Stein and Heinz, *Creativity and the Individual.* Glencoe : The Free Press, 1960.

McKellar, P., "Imagination and Thinking." *Psychol. Analysis,* New York : Basic Books, 1957 : p. 219.

McNemar, Quinn., *Psychological Statistics,* 4th ed., John Wiley and Sons Inc., 1969 : 305-317.

Mednick, S.A., *Remote Association Test,* Boston : Hughton Mifflin, 1967.

Mednic, S.A., and Mednic, M.I., "An Associative Interpretation of the Creative Processes," In C.W. Taylor (ed.), *Widening Horrizons in Creativity,* New York : Wiley, pp. 54-68.

Mednick, S.A., "The Associative Basis of Creative Process." *Psychol. Review,* 1962 : 69, 220-232.

Mooney R.L., "A Conceptual Model for Integration—Four Approaches to the Identification of Creative Talent," in C.W. Taylor (ed.), *The Second (1957) Conference on the Identification of Creative Scientific Talent.* Salt Lake City : University of Ulah Press, 1958 : 170-180.

Mowrer, O.H., "A Stimulus Response Analysis of Anxiety," quoted in W.F. Fischer, *Theories of Anxiety,* Harper and Row, 1970.

Murphy, G., *Human Potentialities.* New York : Basic Books, 1958.

Murray, H.A., "Vicissitudes of Creativity." in H.H. Anderson (ed.), *Creativity and its Cultivation,* New York : Harper 1959, 96-118.

Muller, Braunschweig, Hans., Psychopathology and Creativity in *Psychoanalytic Study of Society* (1975), Vol. 6, 71-99,

Niebuhr, Reinhold, "The Nature and Destiny of Man," quoted in Rollow May, 1950, p. 13.

Osborn, A.F., *Applied Imagination*, New York : Scribners, 1953.

Parnes, S J. "Can creativity be Increased ?," In S.J. Parnes and H.F. Harding (eds.), *A Source Book for Creative Thinking* New York : Scribner's, 1962.

Pathak, P., "Exploratory Study of Creativity and Inrelligence, and Scholastic Achievement." *Psychological Studies*, 1962 : 7, 1-19.

Patel, Kamla., "Profiles of Creative Personality," *Psychologia*, 1976 : 19(4), 173-183.

Perry, John W., "The Creative Element in Madness," *Art Psychotherapy*, 1973 : 1(1), 61-65.

Pickering, G., *The Creative Malady*. New York : Oxford University Press, 1974.

Piotrowski, Lygmunt A., Quoted in H.J. Vetter and B.D., Smith (eds.), *Basic System of all Sciences*, Appllon Century Crofts, New York : 1971, 11-18.

Raina, M.K., "Research on Creative Functioning in India—a Review." *Indian Education Review*, 1972 : 110-115.

— ————, "Research Developments in Creativity in India." *Journal of Research and Development in Education*, 1971 : 4, 118-128.

Raina, M.K., "Study of Reliability and Validity of the Minnesota Tests of Creative Thinking," Unpublished report, University of Indore, 1972.

Raychaudhuri, M., "Personality Correlates of Creativity." *Samiksha*, 1963 : 19, 1707-134.

—— ————, Studies in Artistic Creativity," *Indian Journal of Applied Psychology*, 1966 : 3, 67-70.

————————, and Ganguly, D., "Some Social and Environmental Variables in Creativity." *51st Indian Science Congress*, Part III, 1964.

Rawat, M.S., and Aggarwal, M.B.L., Teaching of Mathematics. (Hindi ed.), Agra : Vinod Pustak Mandir, 244-245.

Roe, Anne., "Personal Problems and Science," in C.W. Taylor, and F. Barron, (eds.), *Scientific Creativity*. John Wiley & Sons, Inc., 1963 : 136.

Roe, Anne., "A Study of Imagery in Research Scientists," *Journal of Personality* XIX (1951) : 459-70.

Roe, Anne, A, Psychological Study of Eminent Psychologists and Anthropologists and a Comparison with Biological and Physical Scientists, *Psychology Monographs*, LXVII No. 2 (1953) : 55.

Rogers, C.R., Towards a Theory of Creativity, A Review of General Semantic XI, 1954, in H.H. Anderson, *Crea ivity and its Cultivation.* New York : Harper, 1959 : 79-82.

Rogers, C.R., *On Becoming a Person.* Boston : Houghton Mfflin Co., 1961 : p. 353.

Roth, N., The Porphyria of H. Heine, quoted in S. Arieti *Creativity—the Magic Synthnsis*, New York : Basic Books, 1976, 357.

Roth, N., Free Association and Creativity, quoted in S. Arieti, *Creativity—The Magic Synthesis*, New York : 1976.

Rouff, L. Lynne., "Openness, Creativity and Complexity," *Psychological Reports*, 1975 : 37, 3 P-1.

SAS Users Guide, 1979 Edition, SAS Instt. Inc., Cary, North CAROLINA.

Schachtel, E.G., *Metamorphoses.* New York : Basic Books, 1959.

Schachtel, E., *Experimental Foundation of Rorschach's* Test. New York : Basic Books, 1959.

Schaefer, C.E. and Anastasi, A., A, Biographical Inventory for Identifying Creativity in Adolescents, quoted in H.J. Eysenck, *The Measurement of Personality*, 1976.

Senter, R.J., *Analysis of Data,* Illinois : Scott, Forseman and Co. 1969.

Simon, Jane., "Creativity and Altered States of Consciousness". *American Journal of Psychoanalysis*, 1977 : 37(1), 3-12.

Spearman, C.E., (1931) quoted in Gowan, Demos and Torrance, *Creativity—Its Educational Implication.* John Wiley and Sons 1967.

Spence, K.W., *Behaviour Theory and Learning.* Englewood Cliffs, N.J. : Prentice Hall, 1956.

Spence, K.W., "Anxiety, Drive level and Performance in Eye lid conditioning," *Psychological Bulletin*, 61, 1964 : 129-39.

Stein, M.I. and Heinze, S.J. (eds.), *Creativity and the Individual.* Free Press of Glencoe, 1960.

Stein, M.I., "Stimulating Creativity." In R.L. Mooney, and T.A. Razik, (eds.), *Exploratians in Creativity*, New York : Harper, 1914.

Stein, S.H. and Harrison, R.H., Conscious and Pre-conscious Influence on Recall. In H.J. Eysenck (ed.), *Readings in Extraversion—Introversion*, London : Staples Press, 1971 : 562.

Suchman, J.R., "Creative Thinking and Conceptual Growth." quoted In Gowan, Demos and Torrance, *Creativity : its Educational Implication*, John Wiley and Sons, 1967 : 134.

Sullivan, H.S., *The Interpersonal Theory of Psychiatry*, New York : Norton, 1953.

Tanwar, R.S., Measurement of Creative Thinking and Their Use in India – An Evaluation of Torrance Tests of Creative Thinking. *Indian Psychological Review*, 1977 : 14, 59-62.

Taylor, C.W., "Some Possible Relations between Expression Abilities and Creative abilities", in C.W. Taylor (ed.), The 1955 University of Utah Conference on Indentification of Creative Scientific Talent Salt Lake City : University of Utah Press, 1956 : 213-18.

Taylor, I.A. "The Nature of Creative Process." In P. Smith (ed.), *Creativity*. New York : Hastings Ho 1959 : 51-82.

Taylor, I.A., "A Retrospective View of Creative Imagination." In I.A. Taylor and J.W. Getzels (eds.), *Perspectives in Creativity*. Chicago : Aldine Publishing Co., 1975.

Taylor, I.A., "The Measurement of Creative Transactualization," *Journal of Creative Behaviour*, 1974 : 8(2), 114-115, 1973.

Thurstone, R.L., The Scientific Study of Inventive Talent, in Parnes, S.J. and H.F. Harding (eds.), *A Source of Book of Creative Thinking*, New York : Scribners 1962, 52.

Tillich, Paul., quoted in Rollo May, *The Meaning of Anxiety*, 1950 : 12.

Torrance. E.P., "Creative Personality and the Ideal Pupil." In Gowan, Demos, and Torrance, *Creativity—Its Educational Implications*, 134, John Wiley and Sons.

Torrance, E P., *Education and the Creative Potential,* University of Minnesota Press, 1962.

Torrance, E.P., "Emerging Concept of Giftedness." In Barbe and Renzulli, *The Psychology and Education of the Gifted.* John Wiley and Sons, 1975 : 51-52.

Torrance, E.P., *Guiding Creative Talent.* New Delhi : Prentice Hall of India Ltd., 1969.

Torrance, E.P., *Rewarding Creative Behaviour,* Englewood Cliff, N.J. : Prentice Hall, Minneapolis, 1965.

Torrance, E.P., Torrance Tests of Creative Thinking, Manual, Princeton, N.J. : Personnel Press, 1966.

Verma, R.S , "A Factor Analytic Study of Divergent Thinking in Relation to Certain Personality dimensions of Higher Secondary School Adolescent." Ph. D. (Ed.) AMU 1973, quoted in M.B. Buch (ed.), *Second Survey of Research in Education.* Baroda : Society for Educational Research and Development, 1979.

Vetter, H.J., and Smith, B.D. (eds), *Personality Theory : Source Book,* New York : Appleton Century Crofts, 1971.

Vinacke, W.E., *The Psychology of Thinking.* New York : McGraw Hill, 1952.

Vos, H.G., "Effect of Experimentally Induced Activation on Creativity." *Journal of Psychology,* 1977 : 96(1), 3-9.

Wallas, G., *The Art of Thought.* New York : Harcourt Brace, 1926.

Walker, Benzamin. *The Hindu World.* London : George Allen and Unwin, 1968.

Wallack, M.A., and Kogan, M , *Modes of Thinking in Young Children.* New Holt Rinehart and Winston, 1965.

Watson, David., "Introversion, Neuroticism, Rigidity and Dogmatism." In H.J. Eysenck (ed.), *Readings in Introversion-Extraversion.* Staff Press, London : 1971 : p. 555.

Weissman, P., "Theoretical Considerations of Ego Regression and Ego Functions in Creativity," *Psychoanalytic Quarterly*, 36, pp. 37-50.

Welsh, G.S. Figure Preference Test, Preliminary Manual, Alto, Calif. Consulting Psychologists Press, 1959.

Wertheimer, M , Productivity Thinking, quoted in 'Silvano Arieti, *Creativity—the Magic Synthesis,* Basic Book 1976 : p. 5.

Zukerman, M., and Spielberger, C.D., *Emotions and Anxiety.* Lawrence—Erlbaum Associates, 1976.

Index

Activation, 57-9
Adualism, 31
Affects *see* Tensions
ANOVA procedures, 121, 122-7t, 128
Anxiety, 4, 17-8, 87-8
  analyses of variance with, 98-110
  causes of, 49-52
  cognitivists' view of, 40-9
  creative thinking and, 131-3
  creatives compared on
    contrast groups, 121, 128-9
  divergent thinking and, 65-7
  Ernest Schachtel's views, 37-8
  experience, 52
  fear and, 35-6, 39-40
  flexibility and, 104t, 106-7
  fluency scores of, 108
  Freud's view of, 34-5
  Horney's views on, 39
  integrative view of, 41-2
  Jacobson's views of, 36-7
  kinds of, 45-7
  meaning of, 32-4
  nature and causes of, 44-9
  neo-Freudian approaches, 35-6
  neuroticism
    relations between, 110-1, 145
  optimal level of, 131-2
  Otto Rank's Views, 38
  positive aspects of, 148-9
  proneness, 133-5, 137-8
  psychoticism
    relations between, 98t, 145-6
  relations with creativity
    nature of, 136-7
  socio-cultural approach to, 39-40
  source of, 41, 44-5
  status of
    creativity and, 135-6
  threshold level of, 131
  types of, 34, 40-1
  univariate statistics for
    sex-wise, 93t-4t, 94-5
  see also Trait-axiety
Architects, 62

Arieti, S , 1, 4, 7-8, 11, 13-4, 24-6, 28-9, 31-3, 40, 130, 143

Aristotle, 49

Arlow, J.A., 15

Arora, G.L., 66-7

Artistic creativity, 63
  personality characteristics of, 63

Averill, J.R., 17, 41

Barron, F., 3, 13, 16, 19, 61-3, 70-3

Bellak, 15

Berkeley University
  studies, 71-3

Binswanger, Luetwig, 26

Bisociation, 23-4

Brenner, C., 15

Bronowski, J., 7

Bruner, J.S., 10

Butcher, H.J., 70

Cattell, R.B., 13, 60-2, 64, 70, 73, 132

Causation, 49-50

Chaudhary, Roy, 63

Chaudhury, Haridas, 6

Chemists, 60

Children, 66, 147-9

Collective Unconscious, 28

Connectedness, 10

Creative process
  phases of, 22
  stages of, 22-3

Creative thinking, 90-1
  anxiety's relations with
    hypotheses of, 131-2, 138
    nature of, 136-7
  anxiety' status and, 135-6
  components of, 68
  dysthemics on, 141
  extraversion and, 139-40
  hysterics on, 141
  neuroticism's relations with, 133-5, 138-9
    nature of, 136-7
    status of, 135-6
  psychoticism and, 142-3
  sex-differences in, 142
  Torrance tests of, 81-3
    scoring, 83-4
  see also Thinking

Creative writings, 64-5

Creativity, 1-2, 16-8
  activation
    empirical studies on, 57-9
  categories, 21-5
  characteristics
    essential, 10-1
  conditions, 9-12
  criterias, 10-11
  definitions of, 6-9
  dogmatism and, 68-9
  emotional factors for, 58-9
  inheritance and, 69, 71
  levels of, 20-1, 28
  mental health and, 13-6, 29, 33

research studies on, 55-7, 59, 69-71
neurotic symptoms and, 55-7
occidentalists' view of, 7-9
orientalists' views of, 6-7
personality studies, 59-69
psychoanalyst's views, 25-32
research studies on, 55-73
sex-differences and, 69
tensions and, 57
theories of
critical review, 20-32

Data
analysis, 92
purposes, 93
collection, 84-5
sample, 84
Dauw, D.C., 67
Discipio, W.J., 140-1
Discipline, 12
Discovery, 7
Divergent thinking, 65-7
see also Creative thinking
Dogmatism
effect of, 68-9
Domino, George, 57
Dıwal, R.L., 58-9
Dreams, 57
Drevdahl, J.E., 60-2, 64, 70-1
Duncan's Multiple Range test, 102-3
for flexibility, 105-7
in neuroticism, 113-5
for fluency, 109-10
for originality, 102-3
in neuroticism, 115
Dutt, N.K., 87-8, 95
Dutt Personality Inventory (DPI), 77-8
Dysthemics, 141, 149

Education, 2, 11-2
Ego, 26-7, 30, 34-7, 61, 63-4, 135-6
regression, 15
Eichbaum, Lange, 14
Elaboration, 83
Emergentive creativity, 21
Emotion, 58-9
Empathy, 36
Expressive creativity, 20
Extraversion, 88
creative thinking and, 139-40
flexibility and, 104
Duncan's test result, 106-7
fluency scores of, 108
original responses of, 103
relationship of
with psychoticism, 98
univariate statistics for
sex-wise, 93t-4t, 94-5
Eysenck, H.J., 53-4, 70, 77, 78-81, 85, 88-9, 95-6, 98, 132, 140-1, 144-5
Eysenck Personality Questionnaire (EPQ), 78-81

Fear, 36, 39-40, 43-4, 51
Female

creativity in, 142
mean scores of
variable-wise, 94t, 94-5
personality dimensions in
relationship between, 97t-8t, 98
Finch, Jeannette M , 66
Findings, 147
Fisher, W.F., 34, 41-2, 45, 145
Flexibility, 90
anxiety's effect on, 132-3
of extraverts, 139-40
GLM procedures for, 104-7
interactions of, 132-3
neuroticism and, 113-5
Fluency, 90, 107-10
anxiety's effects on, 132
of extraverts, 139-40
neuroticism and, 116-7
Frank, 31
Freud, S., 1, 11, 25-6, 29, 33-8, 45
Fromm, Erich, 15, 33, 39-40, 49

General Linear Models procedures
for flexibility, 104-7, 115t
for fluency, 107-10, 117
originality and, 100-1
in neuroticism, 111-3
General psychological, 21-5
Genius
concept of, 3-5
mental illness and
relations of, 13-6
Getzels, W.J., 3
Ghiselin, B., 8
Giftedness, 2-3, 5-6, 11
Gilchrist, 67
Goldstein, 33
Gough, H.G., 60
Gowan, J.C., 1, 16
Greenacre, P., 25, 27
Guilford, J.P., 6, 8, 13, 24, 81, 83

Hallman, R.J., 1, 9-11
Hammer, Emanuel F., 57
Harry, Brand, 55-6
Hebb, 8
Heidegar, 49
Horney, K., 39-40, 49
Human actions, 46
Human creativity *see* creativity
Hysterics, 141, 149

Immediate discovery, 130
Individuation, 33, 38-9
Inferiority anxiety, 45-7
causes of, 50-1
Inheritance, 69, 71
Inhibition-excitation theory, 140
Innovative creativity, 21
Insanity *see* mental health
Introverted neurotics
Invention, 7
Inventive creativity, 20

Jackson, P.W., 3
Jacobson, Edith, 14, 35-7
Jane, 56
Jha, S.K., 63-4, 70-1

Jordon, 53

Jung, C.G., 7, 11, 25, 27-8, 53-4, 63, 141

Kafka, Franz, 55-6

Kandil, Shaker, 66

Kierkegaard, S., 33-4, 49, 134-5

Koestler, Arthur, 23-4

Kogan, M., 8

Kogan, Nathan, 69

Korchin, S.J., 132

Kretchmer, 53-4, 59

Kris, L., 11, 25-7

Krishnamurthi, J., 12

Kubie, L S., 7, 25, 27

Level arousal, 57-9

Levitt, E E., 137

Lie-score scale, 79-80

Linearity, 118, 120

Lombroso, C., 13-4, 29

Mackinnon, D.W., 2-3, 6, 8, 13, 62-3, 72-3, 141

Male
- creativity in, 142
- means score of
  - variable-wise, 94t, 94-5

Manifest Symptonology, 24

Martindale, Colin, 58

Masculinity-femininity scales, 69

Maslow, A H., 3-4, 13, 15, 18, 55, 64

Mathematicians, 62-3

Maudsley Medical Questionnaire (MMQ), 79

Maudsley Personality Inventory (MPI), 79

May, R., 15, 33, 35, 40, 47

McAllister, 70

McKellar, P., 7

McNemar, Quinn, 95, 118, 137

McReynolds, 17-8, 40-1

Measuring scales, 77-8

Mednick, S.A., 8

Mental health
- creativity and, 13-6, 29, 33
  - research studies on, 55-7, 59, 69-71

Mill, J.S., 49

Moral anxiety, 34-5, 45-7
- causes of, 50

Motivational mechanism, 26

Muller-Braunschweig, Hans, 56

Murray, H.A., 8

Needs, 47

Neurotic
- anxiety, 34-5
- symptoms, 55-6

Neuroticism, 79-80, 89
- analyses of variance with, 110-21, 128-9
- anxiety's relations with, 145
- creative thinking and, 133-5, 138-9
- creativity's relations with
  - nature of, 136-7
- curvilinearity of

in relationship, 118-21
flexibility scores of, 104, 106-7
as response variable, 113-5
fluency scores of, 108
as response variable, 116-7
originality in
as response variable, 111-3
rigidity's relations with, 141
status of
creativity and, 135-6
univariate statistics for
sex-wise, 93t-4t, 94-5

Originality, 10, 83-4, 90, 100-5, 147
anxiety and, 136-8
of extraverts, 139
in neuroticism, 111-3
see also Creative thinking

Patel, Kamla, 68
Perry, John W., 56-7
Personality, 19-20
characteristics, 59-65
dimensions of, 52-4
measurement, 78-81
nature, 88-91
orthogonality, 96t-8t, 96-8, 144-5
types, 78
Eysenck's theory of, 141
studies, 59-68
variables
creativity and, 138-9
creative potential and, 68-9
Pervin, 141
Phillipson, 27-8
Pickering, G., 14
Piotrowski, Lygmunt A., 7
Pleasure, 36-7
Potentially Creative persons
personality studies of, 65-8
Primary anxiety, 40-1
Productive creativity, 20, 67
Psychoanalytic, 21-5
Psychological self, 47-8
Psychoneurosis, 13-6
Psychoticism, 70, 87-90, 142-3
anxiety's relations with, 145-6
distributive traits of, 143-4
flexibility score of, 104, 106-7
fluency scores of, 108
reiationship of
with extraversion, 98
scale, 79
Skewed scores of
rationale for using, 95-6
univariate statistics for
sex-wise, 93t-4t, 94-5

Ramanujan, 6
Rank, Otto, 38
Reality
interpretation of, 9
Reality anxiety, 34-5
Regression concept, 27
Reichenback, 31
Research studies, 55-73

Roe, Anne, 59-60, 69
Rogers, C.R., 4, 8, 11, 13, 15
Rossman, 22
Roth, N., 15
Rouf, L. Lynne, 68-9

Safety and security, 4-5
Schachtel, E., 35, 37-8, 47, 49
Schizophrenie, 31-2
School students, 67
Scientific creativity, 59-64
Secondary anxiety, 41
Self-actualization, 18
Senter, R.J., 103
Separation anxiety, 45, 47
  causes of, 51-2
Sex differences, 69, 142
Society, 5
Spence, K.W., 65, 132, 137-8
Spielberger, C.D., 17, 41
Stagnen, 53
Stein, M.I , 8, 13, 23, 60
Study
  design of, 85-7
  hypotheses, 75-7
  purpose, 74-5
Sublimation concept, 25-6
Suchman, J.R., 2
Suggestions, 149-50
Sullivan, H.S., 35-6

Taft, 67
Talentedness, 2-3
Taylor, I.A , 8, 16, 20-1, 61
Tensions, 37
Tertiary process, 8
Thinking, 6, 8
  divergent, 24
  see also Creative thinking
Thurstone, R.L., 8
Tillich, Paul., 33
Torrance, E P., 3, 6, 13, 16, 66, 81-4, 90
Torrance Tests of Creative Thinking (TTCT), 81-3
  scoring of, 83-4
Trait-anxiety, 77
  measuring inventory for, 77-8
Tripathi, 64-5
Twain, Mark, 2
Type, 53

Unconsciousness
  role in creativity, 55-7
Unconcious mental operations, 10-11

Vos, H.G., 57-8

Wallach, M.A., 8
Wallas, G., 22
Watson, David, 141, 143
Weissman, P., 25, 27
Wertheimer, M , 23-4
White, Kinnard, 65-6, 139

Yamamoto, 82
Yerkes-Dodson Law, 137
Yogin, 6-7

Zukerman, M., 41